The Homemade Beer Book

D1714258

The Homemade BEER BOOK

In Which are included General Principles
and Recipes for Making Beer in the Home,
History of Beer, Drinking Customs of
Old New England, Brewing of the
Olden Times, Curious Lore of
Oldtime Brewing, Etc., Etc.

By *VREST ORTON*
Author of "Vermont Afternoons with Robert Frost"

CHARLES E. TUTTLE COMPANY
Rutland, Vermont

Representatives

Continental Europe: BOXERBOOKS, INC., *Zurich*

British Isles: PRENTICE-HALL INTERNATIONAL, INC., *London*

Australasia: BOOK WISE (AUSTRALIA) PTY. LTD.
104-108 Sussex Street, Sydney 2000

Canada: HURTIG PUBLISHERS, *Edmonton*

Published by the Charles E. Tuttle Company, Inc.
of Rutland, Vermont & Tokyo, Japan
with editorial offices at
Suido 1-chome, 2-6, Bunkyo-ku, Tokyo, Japan

Copyright in Japan, 1973 by Charles E. Tuttle Co., Inc.

Library of Congress Catalog Card No. 72-89742

International Standard Book No. 0-8048-1086-9

First Tuttle edition, 1973
Third printing, 1976

PRINTED IN JAPAN

INTRODUCTION TO THE NEW EDITION

FORTY YEARS AGO the blight of the National Prohibition Law lay heavy upon the land. Perhaps, in the 200-year span of American history, no federal law was more resented, less observed, and in the end as fatal to the high principles of law and order in the United States. The winds of discontent with this law and the overt flouting of it were phenomena of that racy decade ending in 1933. Today, of course, we are reaping the wildwind.

Libraries devote shelves of weighty and even frivolous tomes written since that dire era to delineate and explain the legal, social, economic, moral, ethical, and other polluting results that this frightful and, as it was called, "noble" experiment generated in our country.

The Homemade Beer Book is not one of these tomes!

Let me make it very clear at the outset: this is a reprint of a book privately printed and issued in 1932. The first edition has become one of the rarest volumes of the Prohibition epoch. Copies, and there have been few, that reached the market have fetched up to $150 each. Under its original title (reproduced on page 5), *Proceedings of the Company of Amateur Brewers,* it was printed forty years ago and limited to 300 copies.

Members of the select group who owned the book, were they alive today, would find this fact somewhat amusing, because this original edition was never published in the legal sense and therefore was never sold. It was given free to members in good standing of a small group called the Company of Amateur Brewers.

How did such a state of affairs come about?

First, the *Proceedings,* like the proceedings of any other scholarly society, were gathered and set into type as a result of the deliberations and experiments of a few kindred souls. With wit, much work, and considerable patience these men saw to it, in the last years before the Prohibition era ended, that they were not obliged, like most of their benighted fellow citizens of that sad time, to suffer the loss of alcoholic beverages, notably good beer.

No such formal culmination of our experiments as *The Proceedings* was dreamt of when, in the beginning, a few of us began figuring out ways and means of making decent potable beer in the home. But as time went on, some of the members with a historical bent and scholarly equipment were interested in going deeper into the subject than mere recipes for home brewing. As a result, the papers in *The Proceedings* were placed in the hands of the members who, at the height of membership, never numbered but a few kindred spirits.

Frankly, I do not know if any members are alive today. Membership records, like much ephemera of that time forty years back, have been lost. For some years after 1932 I kept in touch, but the lines were tenuous, and after the Prohibition amendment was repealed and legal beer flowed onto the market, the interest waned.

However, I had better say for the record that I was Master of the Company and embraced the literary *nom de plume* of A. P. Wallace. Why I did this I can't rightly remember now. Certainly it was not because of fear of the law. The printing of recipes for making beer was perfectly legal, just so long as such were not offered for sale on the open market. No copy of *The Proceedings* was ever offered for sale by the company. The real reason for the name Wallace probably lay more in the fact that when I was very, very young I had committed the indiscretion of writing and, what is worse, allowing to be published a certain body of work that passed for poetry but was not, I believe, even very good verse. And all this was under the name A. P. Wallace.

The Homemade Beer Book is a complete reprint without omissions but with one exception: in the chapter on modern brewing recipes, I have made a few minor changes to bring matters up to date and to recommend a national source of supply for paraphernalia and ingredients necessary to the art of making good beer in the home.

I do know one thing: every one of the speakers of this illustrous group, the transcripts of which follow here, is now dead. Since I am the last one alive, it falls upon me, as a sacred duty, to allow my old friend Charles Tuttle to reissue this rare tome in a new format so that it may come within the reach today of many instead of a privileged few, as it did forty years ago.

Vrest Orton

Weston, Vermont

NOTES ON MODERN EQUIPMENT & SUPPLIES

Please read before using recipes in this book.

OBVIOUSLY while paraphernalia and supplies we employed forty years ago in brewing beer are often the same today, some are no longer available, and in all cases prices have no relation to those of former times. In the two chapters devoted to methods and recipes for modern brewing there are several references to establishments purveying equipment and supplies. On page 61 I note that malt syrup was selling in 1930 for as low as 45 cents a can, and on page 67 it says that dry hops could be bought for 25 cents a package! Those were the days when a man could buy a good dress shirt for $2.00 and unskilled labor fetched $1.00 a day. Clerks in department stores earned as much as $15.00 per week.

Rather than correct with bothersome footnotes the references to supplies, equipment, and prices throughout the book, I will mention a national mail order house called Wine-Art of America. The only thing I know about these people is the comprehensive and attractive mail-order catalog they put out in which seems to be listed every conceivable item a man would ever need in the making of beer as well as of wine. There are many other purveyors of brewing products throughout the United States, but these people are apparently the only ones who list over fifty branches in all parts of the country. A letter to this firm at 4324 Geary Boulevard, San Francisco, California 94118, will bring you the addresses of their branches and a catalogue. I list this outfit only because of the convenience of their service.

I should add that today there are many more ingredients for brewing beer than there were in 1930. You will find several kinds of yeasts, malt syrups and extracts, finings and filters, and other supplies to give you a wide choice of brews you can make in the home. Forty years ago, for example, the fresh "yeast cake" was the only yeast available. Today there are special brewing yeasts, and, I believe, dried yeast is sold in all markets.

As to brewing supplies, there have been changes, most for the better. Except in an antique shop, no longer can you buy the copper wash boiler referred to on page 69. I suppose I should explain that once upon a time clothes were boiled before being washed! A "crock" probably needs another explanation. Once used by farm-wives to put down pickles, salt pork, or eggs, and by us during Prohibition to make beer, these big heavy earthenware utensils are still around but not in every department store. There are several sizes of professional stainless-steel stock pots, with covers, used by restaurants, that will serve as well in beer making. Finings and filters other than isinglass are available, but the old-time milk skimmer mentioned on page 84 is indeed a relic of the past, although stainless-steel skimmers are on the market. I recommend that you ignore the reference on page 87 to supply houses in business forty years ago.

If smirking wine be wanting here,
There's that which drowns all care,
Stout beere.

HERRICK

INTERIOR OF AN ANCIENT BREWHOUSE

PROCEED-INGS OF THE COMPANY

OF

Amateur Brewers

Dulce est desipere in loco

Privately printed in 1932 for the
MEMBERS of THE SOCIETY

CONTENTS

Privately Printed for Members

❧ PROLEGOMENA. By The Secretary of The Company, in his capacity as General Editor of the Proceedings; printed by the order of the Master, March, 1932.

THE gathering and printing of the several addresses delivered before the Annual, Special, and Monthly Meetings of *The Company*, mark a new departure in the policy of this Society. The move was instituted by a formal vote of the members assembled at the last Annual Meeting, holden October first, 1931, in order that members, particularly new members, might have a permanent record of the mass of material which otherwise would not be preserved. I have the honor to present these printed *Proceedings*, hoping they may be the first of a long series.

Two addresses, I regret to report, were printed without their respective authors having had the opportunity to examine proofs. I refer to the addresses of the Hon. David L. MacIntosh and Major Ethan K. Stevens. Mr. MacIntosh was called to Washington two days before the meeting to accept an appointment to *The International Bureau of*

Prohibition Statistics, which necessitated his paper being read by the Secretary. Before the address was set in type, Mr. MacIntosh sailed for Italy on a mission for the *Bureau* and could not be reached. Major Stevens's paper on modern recipes, read by him before the Monthly Meeting, was also not submitted to its author for final checking of the proofs. With the deepest regret I must report that Major Stevens was taken ill while journeying to his home in Boston and died suddenly two days later of angina pectoris at a hospital. Major Stevens's death, which, needless to say, is a great shock to all members of *The Company,* is a tremendous loss to us as well as to his military associates.

Major Stevens's life has been one of great distinction and many honors. He served with gallantry in the Spanish American War in Cuba, commanding a company in the 10th cavalry. He was mentioned in dispatches in this campaign and twice later in the Philippine Insurrection where he was promoted from Captain to Major. During the World War, Major Stevens accepted a commission in the Canadian Army in 1915, but in action at St. Quentin was wounded in the arm, which necessitated an amputation and his being retired from active service. For extraordinary bravery in this engagement he was awarded the Military Cross by the English. In 1923 the Distinguished Service Medal was awarded by the American Government, a belated honor long due him. At the last Special Meeting, Mr. A. P. Wallace, our Master, read the following tribute:

> It is with a profound personal feeling of sadness and loss that I speak here of the death of our beloved fellow member and friend, Major Ethan K. Stevens. We who have had the pleasure of continued association with this distinguished gentleman since the founding of *The Company* can vouch in no uncertain words for the sincere esteem and unqualified respect we all felt for him. It is thus a sad duty but one

embellished with honor, that I, as Master of this Society, do hereby cause these few and feeble words to be inserted in the *Proceedings* as our tribute to the memory of this best of companions and finest of scholars, Ethan K. Stevens.

I know Major Stevens, if he had lived, would have been wholly satisfied with the accuracy of the transcription of his address by Mr. Norman E. Bronson, editor of the NORTHERN FOLK-LORE ARCHIVES who kindly consented to read proofs.

The papers which follow are printed *seriatim et verbatim* since it was thought best to eliminate all editing, that the *Proceedings* might exhibit a complete and accurate record of the several addresses as they were delivered. Repetitions will doubtless be observed but the effect *in toto* should compensate for minor shortcomings of this nature.

It must be said, as a final word, that 1931 has witnessed a new and highly encouraging coöperation among members, which fact can only denote the increasing strength of the organization. The influence of the Society is being felt in many quarters and the printing of its trans-actions should accentuate the benefits of its good work. On behalf of myself and the officers of *The Company* I want to ask all new members to rally to the support of measures calculated to increase the member-ship of proper persons in this Society. I wish also to record here the thanks and appreciation of the entire membership to all who have so kindly allowed their private records to be searched for the data now incorporated in the addresses printed in this volume.

THE ORIGIN & AIMS OF THE COMPANY OF AMATEUR BREWERS. The Opening Address before the Annual Meeting, October 1, 1931. By A. P. Wallace, Master of The Company.

Blessed is he that hath lived well and ended happily.
—Thomas à Kempis

ENTLEMEN: It is a pleasure to welcome the motion of our Senior Warden to open our membership rolls to other kindred spirits. Up to now, selfishly I fear, we have confined to our exclusive group the great body of fact that has come out of our experiments and deliberations. I believe that the world has pressing need of good spirit and good beer such as we have indulged in, and I am glad to know that new "kinsprits" will soon be numbered among us. But these new friends cannot be kindred in spirit and festive in companionship until they are aware of the aims and purposes of *The*

Company of Amateur Brewers, or until they know something of the spirit that has animated and will continue to animate us and keep us in mutual harmony. It is then my duty, as titular head of this organization, to speak of these matters and to give some inkling of what we have done and what we hope to do.

We were originally drawn together by one great compelling thirst in common. This is plain. But there was more. Up here in Vermont, where *The Company* started, a corner of the land once noted for its independence, we still hold to a vestige of that quality so rare in the modern world. I refer, of course, to a love of liberty. We Vermonters used (when we were a separate sovereignty, free from the shackles of the Crown and likewise from those of the unorganized colonies) to do as the spirit moved us. We hewed our way through the forests; we built outposts of civilization; we chastized the Yorkers who wanted our land; we made the first capture of a fortress in the Revolution; we set off audaciously to take the impregnable Montreal with a mere handful of men, half a hundred; we did, in short, pretty much as free men are wont to do. Those days are gone, but not the spirit that moved us. The spirit, we feel, has coursed down through the blood of generations and we are proud to love and honor the virtues of independence and liberty. Out of this spirit was born *The Company of Amateur Brewers.* When the time came to take matters into our own hands; when we knew there was not at hand the satisfaction of our mutual thirst, we took to improving the situation. We took to getting the things we wanted. This was the origin of *The Company.*

Eleven dour years have passed since the advent of our country's noble prohibitory regulations. During this doleful decade, the art of brewing has changed . . . in fact it has progressed in an entirely opposite direction. It has witnessed from the beginning a movement from the hands of private to those of commercial brewers, and now it has come back into the confines of the home. Everybody knows something of that horrible pandemic—the industrial revolution—that leapt upon us in the nineteenth century. That calamity put a stop to many pleasant factors of a not too unhappy existence. Definitely, and as one was beginning to think permanently, this universal upheaval in ways of living and working, checked the growth of the craft spirit among men and, in fact, snuffed out entirely the pleasant art of domestic manufacture. But this was only the surface and tangible result of the revolution. For more disastrous and profound results, I refer you to the present depression, the recent war, the plight of the individual in this civilization of robots, etc., etc. But of all this, one thing concerns us. Of the many products that were once made with loving care by men's hands, in men's homes, BEER, glory be, is one of the few that has outlived the blight of that revolution; one that has triumphed over mass production and one that contains a ray of hope toward a solution of our difficulties in this century! For this we are thankful. Maybe, in encouraging and promoting the brewing of good beer in the homes of our reputable citizens, we are in the vanguard of a new movement toward individualism and toward the salvage of good qualities from the simpler days of yesteryear. Those days, I mean, when the common man, as well as the artisan and the aesthete, did fine things for themselves, one thing at a time, under their own rooftrees, as their own employers—and took a pride in it, too!

Well, that's what we want. Contrasted with the drab serial production assembly line in a Ford factory of today, where each man is an integral part of the machine, the individual, free spirit of the eighteenth century in arts and crafts is to be admired. We do admire it. That is the reason we wish to emulate it. That is the reason why we have formed this small group, now to grow larger, in order to investigate and work out better and more enjoyable ways of doing things ourselves.

The rolls of *The Company of Amateur Brewers* are open to good men and true, because if there be more men who believe as we do, we want to associate with them. We want the benefit of their companionship and their knowledge. We have another feeling, although this is not subscribed to by all our members. I refer to the astounding fact that the brewing and imbibing of good beer is a pleasure almost wholly confined to the male of the species. Among us are no out-and-out misogynists, and we do not believe in issuing any manifesto on the subject, but truly it seems a great consolation to us that puny man may at last endulge in one *exclusive* pleasure. It is not that we, as men, are jealous or resentful of our lovely counterparts. But man is a lazy creature! There are times, many times, when he feels the strain of polite society, when he would escape from the charming necessities of being on his good behavior before the delightful creatures who often demand good behavior. These are the times when he wishes to retire with a group of "kinsprits" and drink beer. The female, for the most part, is willing to allow him to do this, as she does not apparently love that noble beverage. Thus we have our place cut out for us. We know where we can escape. The brewing and drinking, in masculine society, of good beer, is our last frontier, our last refuge. Let us make the most of it! We may never have another.

But, my dear brothers, I would not have you assume that the drinking or brewing of beer is a vulgar pursuit. Far from it! The brewing of beer, as you may learn from the address of Mr. MacIntosh boasts of a long and noble history, full of honor and the benefits of classic antiquity. Long before the seeds that were to start the first vine of the grape in France were germinated, pleasant beer was being drunk with relish. Long before the invention of spirits which besotted the dark ages, mild beer was being enjoyed by the Greeks, Romans, Egyptians and Teutons. A long and honorable lineage of poets has sung in praise of beer. That beer inspired much is recognized by us all personally, and everybody is aware how the nobleman of the past doted upon his private and special brew of beer. Even today, the Prince of Wales has his special brew, as do other gentlemen in Britain, where the art of brewing still flourishes. Beer, in short, is the drink of gentlemen. It is, however, more than a drink. It is a food. It is the only beverage of high nutritious value which at the same time exhilarates and inspires, and is favourable to the taste of men. Beer is the drink of the Anglo-Saxon and the Teuton, primarily. Its mild and beneficial qualities appeal to these men. *The Company of Amateur Brewers* has the notion that the world could well employ many of the fine human qualities that are emphasized by the mild tonic of good beer.

There have been raised some questions about an important influence on the activities of *The Company*. I refer to the Laws. Well, it seems that the paternal federal government has announced a policy of great benefit to all. The department of justice, where the enforcement of the prohibition laws now reposes, has stated that a policy of hands off will be pursued when the product of the vats or presses is for home consumption and not for sale. Further, it must be borne in mind that no persons, agents or others, can enter private homes without due warrant, fully describing the material to be seized, unless they break in and thus violate every meaning and purpose of the Federal Constitution of these United States. The clause in this great document is quite plain;

"the right of the people to be secure in their persons, houses, papers and effects against unreasonable searches and seizures, shall not be violated and no Warrants shall issue, but upon probable cause, supported by Oath or affirmation and particularly describing the place to be searched and the persons or things to be seized."

The founding fathers wrote good, plain English. If this English means what it says, then all members of *The Company of Amateur Brewers* may brew fine beers in their homes for domestic and personal use, and may do so under the benevolent aegis of our central government.

There is another important factor of common interest. Since 1920 many sad things have happened to our ales and beers. The first few years of the plague, no potable ale or beer could easily be secured. And very few persons had come upon the art of concocting them in small quantities in the homes. The result was chaos. Professional bootleggers began devising the most horrible mixtures with only one purpose in mind: to create a liquid not for pleasant taste, for fine colour or for congeniality . . . not for the good of the stomach, the head, or the soul, but merely, hark you, for the highest possible alcoholic content! All manner of incredible potions were manufactured from every conceivable substance. And some utterly inconceivable. These distillers, with crude apparatus, and cruder minds, are today shouldered with a tremendous responsibility for crime, disease, maiming of the population, disregard of good laws—in fact for the deaths of thousands of citizens poisoned by the spirits that issued from their wretched distilleries.

Such a responsibility should make for little sleep o' nights. And a responsibility almost as great is that which now must weigh upon the gentlemen responsible for prohibition.

For years, as I say, no decent beer emerged. Beer was made, it is true, but it was insulted by being "spiked" or fortified with alcohol. And often with ether and other drugs. To give a kick, mind you! Certainly beer, that noble food, that most nutritious liquid, touched its lowest ebb in those days. The fortified product was obviously not for men of wisdom and manners. Such would have nothing to do with it. That is why they retired to their cloisters. Now, during the last three years results have come from the cloisters. Our *Company,* as an organized group of loyal and congenial souls, caused a gentleman's drink to come into being. Beer of decent content is what I mean, and this is what is now being made in the homes of our members. And beer as good and as pleasant as yesterday's departed, brown October!

For, as a matter of fact, the new brew-masters who have developed a technique under the special conditions of small volume production now know what the old masters always knew . . . that beer too strong is as bad as beer too anæmic. The fine old beers of the other day . . . the beers one could drink all day long, and half through the night—the Pilsner, the Münchner, the Berlin Dark—were never actually strong, knock-you-in-the-head beers such as the weighted Irish product or the 9% English Stout. These fine old beers were just right. They enabled one to be a gentleman, a scholar and often a god. They were the beers that inspired the ego, tickled the soul, routed the repressions and were chock full of the vigor, the gusto and the beauty of living!

My dear brothers, I begin to wax sentimental. This is a good stop-sign. But not without one more word. Those who would mix their congeniality with the pleasant atmosphere of *The Company of Amateur Brewers,* should by all means understand that *The Company* has one great purpose. It is to make better and better the fine beers I have been talking about and never, never, never to fortify beer, or try to make an imitation of that most potent sledge hammer product that was enough to keep the Middle Ages dark. For men of sense and feeling good beer is good beer. The data in the proceedings of the society is contrived to help attain the end of good beer. The recipes included are the result of accurate and careful experiment. You can do this and that—you can add raisins or wheat or whatnot to the wort and think you improve matters. But you do not. If you follow instructions carefully and keep the basic rule of cleanliness always in mind, you will have as good and fine a beer as our forefathers enjoyed. And that, dear brothers of the vat, is what you want, or you would not be members of this illustrious *Company*. For *The Company of Amateur Brewers* is founded on a simple quality—good fellowship. It is held together by pleasant talk, amiable manners, mutual purposes and a good frothy mug of cold beer at every elbow. I thank you.

❧ A BEER VIEW OF HISTORY. An Address before the Annual Meeting, October 1, 1931. By The Hon. David L. MacIntosh, M. C. (Read by the Secretary.)

Wer nicht liebt Wein, Weib, und Gesang,
Der bleibt ein Narr sein Leben lang.
—credited to LUTHER

MR. WALLACE, OFFICERS OF THE COMPANY, FELLOW MEMBERS: It may interest us, met here tonight, to learn a little of the noble and ancient lineage of the beverage to which we do honor in our gatherings. You know a great deal about the excellence of beer, its nutritive and medicinal virtues and methods of brewing. All of this is essential to a proper appreciation of the liquid that has been beloved of man since the dawn of civilization. But to value it at its true worth you must realize the part beer has played in the history of mankind, not only in affecting the destinies of nations, but in influencing those social relations without which we would be on a level with the brutes.

When Egypt was at its zenith, brewing had acquired such a high degree of skill that its origin must have been thousands of years earlier. Egyptian beer, called *heqa,* was made of barley and, as the priests and nobles relished a good brew, the temples and estates had brew-houses where scrupulous care was taken in its manufacture. Herodotus credits the introduction of brewing to the goddess Isis, and the most celebrated Egyptian beer was made near her temple at Pelusium, about twelve hundred years before the birth of Christ.

The Egyptians, the sophisticates of their age, were Epicurians who lived on the best the world afforded. Like all self-sufficient and sophisticated peoples, they despised foreigners. You can picture a Pharaoh majestically enthroned while receiving a Babylonian or Assyrian ambassador, or a Numidian or Ethiopian prince. He doubtless felt like one of our earlier presidents when Chief Kicking Antelope of the Cheyennes came to Washington to see the Great White Father. When the barbarian had offered his lavish presents and had come to the point of negotiating a treaty or seeking the hand of a princess for his sovereign, he would be entertained with all the resources of the royal palace. While an ancient version of the Follies was performed, the Pharaoh and his guest would whet their enjoyment by quaffing the royal brew. These entertainments usually took a long time and the regal tankard would be emptied again and again. At the end of the show, king and ambassador were in that mellow state where one can begin to believe in the brotherhood of man. As a consequence the business was transacted satisfactorily and Egypt was saved from the jealously and aggressions of her rivals for a few years more. Some day a learned Egyptologist will find that beyond the shadow of a doubt Egypt's decline started when its brewers no longer maintained the standard of their product.

I will not say much about the brews of the Assyrians, Chaldeans and Babylonians. These nations were just as barbarous as the Egyptians thought them. It is true that they contributed to sculpture, architecture, literature and law, but these are only the trappings of civilization. The bas-reliefs dug up by archaeologists show these curly-bearded, hook-nosed Semites flaying live captives and indulging in other abominable atrocities impossible to a people mellowed by good beer. Even their monstrous gods seem the creations of minds inflamed by a liquor of the highest voltage. I therefore present the thesis that they were consumers of liquids fully as potent as bath-tub gin and that they scorned the mild effects of beer.

When they first entered the historical spotlight the Medes and Persians were vastly superior to the people in the city-states south of them. Later they lost their old virtues and adopted elegant and effete Oriental manners and vices. It was then that the Greeks, nurtured on brews they had learned about from the Egyptians, showed that a handful of indomitable beer drinkers could overcome the greatest of empires when it had forsaken the contents of the brewing vats for exotic and befuddling liquors. In their beer drinking heyday the Persians were invincible, but they succumbed to the inebriate habits of the nations they conquered. Originally beer had played such a prominent part in their lives, and so many virtues had been ascribed to its use, that in later centuries it was known as MEAD, an evident corruption of MEDE. I am aware that this derivation is not accepted by all etymologists, but who cares?

The Greeks likewise acquired a taste for strange and potent drinks, and when their desire for beer departed so did "the glory that was Greece." Alexander the Great, had he never been tempted from his boyhood brews by the deadly concoctions of the Persians, would in all probability have added India and China to his conquests instead of dying a drunkard's death at thirty-three. Archilochus, Dioscorides,

Sophocles, Xenophon and Aristotle all mention the Hellenic addiction to beer. On the other hand, the modern Greeks, whose blood is infused with that of Turks, Bulgars and various eastern races, may owe their present lowly status to their renunciation of beer for *douziko,* familiar to the Turks as *raki.* This colorless liquor, cool enough to look at, is burning as hell-fire and powerful as dynamite. Whether the Turks introduced this high explosive potable in an effort to kill off the Greeks or *vice versa* I do not know. Another tenable theory is that the Athenians, with characteristic guile, invented *douziko* as a poison for their enemies and so originated the phrase. "I fear the Greeks when they come bearing gifts."

Beer never played as prominent a part in the lives of the Romans as did the wines praised in rhapsodic verse by Latin poets. The pre-empire Roman was a stern, practical man of affairs, an imperialist who believed in his divine mission to force his *mores* on inferior peoples. During the republic Rome was too busy with internecine strife and wars with Carthage and the Gauls to have the leisure for luxurious living. Luxury came later and with it began the decline and fall of *Roma Imperatrix.* The beer drinkers were too strong for her.

Pliny writes learnedly of the use of beer in Spain and Gaul. After the Romans occupied these countries they did much to improve the native brews. When the Romans pushed on into Britain they found the inhabitants brewing ale from barley and wheat. Under Roman tutelage the quality of British brews increased rapidly.

The Teutonic races who eventually usurped more than their fair share of the earth after turning back Caesar's vaunted legions, were beer-swiggers notable for their love of liberty. Tacitus comments on both the brews and the independence of the German tribes. These Teutons were the progenitors of our own colonial settlers. Our devotion to beer and liberty have been bequeathed to us by the sea-rovers who followed Hengist and Horsa into England. Let us protect those heritages that should be sacred to us!

Only among the Germanic nations and their cousins the Scandinavians has beer reached the full flower of perfection. Wine is delightful, uplifting the soul and filling it with the *joie de vivre*. It quickens the emotions and causes man to see the world as tinged with its own roseate hue. It inspires flights of fancy, has added much to the poetry of living, and is to be commended as a drink that makes men and women look upon one another kindly. There is an aesthetic appeal to wine: it has a beauty of color, a sparkle, that endears it to women. It provides gayety and zest, but about it there is something feminine and soft as opposed to the masculine qualities of beer. There is just that difference between the Latin and Teutonic races that you find in wine and beer. If you have ever tasted French or Italian beer, a ghastly parody of a worthy brew, you will understand that the genius of a people must surely be embodied in the liquors it makes and drinks.

When the Angles, Saxons and Jutes made England their own they brought the secrets of their brews with them and quickly adopted all the "tricks of the trade" that the decamped Romans had left behind. They considered beer an essential food as necessary as bread, and during the turbulent period when Danes, Norwegians and Normans were harrying the country the stubborn English continued to make their beer.

The Vikings were also beer drinkers of magnificent capacity. Among them a man's prowess was measured by his skill with sword and battle-axe and his ability to out-drink his companions. The *sagas* allude to convivial occupations as often and as dithyrambically as they do to feats of arms. These enormous flaxen-haired fighters spent the long northern nights listening to the songs of scop and gleeman, while silver-banded horns were filled with foaming beer and emptied without pause. Their idea of heaven, which they called Valhalla, was a place where they could fight and carouse eternally, drinking limitless beer from the skulls of their foes.

Every schoolboy knows that the Vikings were the first Europeans to reach America and that they named it Vinland because of the profusion of wild grapes. They left a small force of colonists on the coast, but no trace of them was ever found. Now I have an idea as to what happened to these first settlers. They ran out of beer and, since they had no ingredients for brewing they made wine from the abundant grapes. When the intensely cold weather came and the Indians raided them they tried to sustain their spirits with fermented grape juice. The unfamiliar drink failed to cheer them. They finally missed their beer so much they thought life not worth living. While they fought the *Skraelings* (as they called the redskins) their minds were diverted by longing for beer. They preferred death at the hands of savages to a bitter winter without their inspiriting brews.

When the Normans invaded France and occupied Normandy they were typical beer drinking Vikings, but it did not take them long to acquire a veneer of Latin culture. By the time they conquered England they had the French liking for wine. Their wine bibbing propensity

was a recent acquisition, but love of beer was "bred in the bone." When the various people in Britain had been fused into one race, the English devotion to malt liquors became a national characteristic.

During the Middle Ages the brewing of beer and ale in England prospered mightily. Some of the greatest and best breweries were connected with monasteries. The brothers of the cowl toiled from dawn to dark raising barley, experimenting with different brews and bringing their "brown October" to a perfection celebrated in mediæval ballads. The Church encouraged good living. The monks of England were as famed for their beers and ales as the Trappists and Benedictines have been for their *liqueurs* in recent years. Tonsured friar, hunted outlaw and belted earl had in common their gustatory affection for "nut brown ale."

It might be well to explain at this point that English brews before the sixteenth century were ales made from malted barley alone. Beer (from the German word *bier*) differs from ale in having an infusion of hops. The introduction of beer into England from Flanders in 1524 is commemorated in the couplet:

> *Turkies, carp, picarell, and beere,*
> *Came into England all in one year.*

This distinction in nomenclature no longer holds good, except that the term ale is not used for stout, porter or lager beer.

The most famous of the old English brews was Burton ale from Burton-on-Trent. A local monk found that the waters of the river Trent, running over rocks of gypsum, contained an unusually large proportion of sulphate of lime, together with carbonate and muriate of lime, and had remarkable properties that caused ales brewed from it to become bright and clear almost immediately. These early discoveries led to the knowledge that the character of the water (technically called *liquor*) is a most important factor, and that the best water must not be heavy with organic matter. Burton beer, a bitter ale, is a product of the hard water of the Trent, but for most brews soft "water from the skies" is desirable. It has been said that "water which makes good tea makes good beer."

As the monasteries dwindled in number and importance brewing came more and more into the hands of laymen. Every gentleman had his own beers and ales made in the brew house that had become an essential building on all estates. The poorer folk concocted their brews at home, and in the cities Companies were formed to satisfy the thirst of the townsmen. Those were the days when each craft had its guild "for the support of the body and the salvation of the soul," to regulate the practise of its art and guard its secrets. The Brewers Company became a strong member of the London Companies and gave impetus to what has become one of England's greatest industries. The commercial brewers or "brewers for sale" at first brewed beers and ales for the common people only, as the gentry relied on their private brew houses. This gradually changed and the habit of special and personal brews is today held only amongst the privileged few who appreciate the fundamental spirit of the craft and are suspicious of mass production.

The discomforts inseparable from life before the invention of modern conveniences were mitigated by "jolly good ale and old." No matter how humble the traveller he was sure of welcome and cheer at any inn where he could spend a penny for liquid refreshments. Hospitality was general throughout "the tight little isle." The guest who entered a home or tavern was regaled with food and drink. Tankards of the host's favorite brews contributed to his delectation. Under the expansive influence of beer men warmed to each other and became the best of good fellows. The taciturn man grew loquacious and the talkative individual was inspired to new eloquence. Over the brimming flagons affairs of state were settled; alliances between families were consummated; old animosities were forgotten; eternal friendships were sworn and sorrows were drowned. Beer made the English a cohesive people—hale, hearty and indomitable.

The upper classes in England decreased their consumption of beer as they had increasingly steady and intimate contact with the continent. Wines became the beverage of the fashionable and were forced to compete for favor with whiskies and, in recent years, "the pernicious cocktail." Even now the aristocracy still like their beers and ales, although they drink far less of them than they used to, but to the middle classes and the great mass of working people the output of the breweries remains as popular as ever. The English "pub" is an accepted institution and English beers and ales are pure and wholesome. The Englishman continues to believe that "his home is his castle," and woe betide any snooper who tries to intrude on the liberties of a free-born Briton. Beer of sorts has been the drink of old England since the Druids sacrificed at Stonehenge, and when there is no more beer there will be no more England.

The colonists who settled the American coast from Maine to Florida were for the most part of pure English stock. The Puritans of New England held views entirely different from those of the people below the Mason and Dixon line, but they all agreed in their love of beer and spirituous liquors. Puritanism was never synonymous with prohibition. The founders of Massachusetts were frequenters of tap rooms and there exist tavern bills for "the entertainment of the ministers" on which the prinicpal items are for liquors supplied to the bibulous divines.

The earliest records of beer in America are found in the writings of the Pilgrim Fathers. When the Pilgrims put ashore their first landing party near Provincetown they had their initial drink of American water from a spring. The contemporary chronicle relates, rather naïvely, that in their exhaustion they found it "as pleasant unto them as wine and beer had been in foretime." Again, in Plymouth, when seeking the most suitable townsite, Mourt wrote that "we could not now take time for further search or consideration, our victuals being much spent, especially our beer." A little later Governor Bradford complained loudly and frequently against the scarcity of good beer in the colony.

For a few years the colonists were forced to import their beer from England, but in 1637 one Captain Sedgewick opened the first colonial brewery, in Boston. The settlers had probably brewed some beer in their homes previous to this, as many of them must have been accustomed to making their own brews in England. It was not long before "kill-devil" or New England rum was the common drink of the northern colonies and families became wealthy through the importation of the molasses used in its manufacture, as well as by supplying the better grade of rum from Jamaica. But despite bountiful and cheap hard liquors there was a predilection for beer that could not be satisfied because of the scarcity of competent brewers and high quality malt. The use of make-shift substitutes is indicated in a stanza which goes something like this:

> *If barley be wanting to make into malt,*
> *We must be content and think it no fault,*
> *For we can make liquor to sweeten our lips,*
> *Of pumpkins, and parsnips, and walnut-tree chips.*

Communities were so anxious to get good beer that they offered special inducements to brewers to settle in their midst. In Massachusetts the legislative body offered tax immunity and a money prize to any brewer producing more than five hundred barrels of "honest beer" in a year, not only to aid prosperity by giving the farmers an improved market for their barley, but also to discourage the drinking of "strong waters."

The tap rooms of the old inns were the gathering places of the men who lived near by. Here neighborhood gossip was exchanged, politics were discussed and business was carried on. As ever, beer and liberty went hand-in-hand, and it was at the taverns that patroits met and formed their plans for resisting tyranny. George III, a German who should have known better, tried to coerce a nation of beer drinkers. The exponents of independence flocked to arms, forced Europe to recognize the free United States, and then returned to their peaceful pastime of drinking beer. They assumed that they had vindicated their right, and that of their posterity forever, to indulge their inclination for beer without molestation. If only they could see the sad plight of their supine descendants!

During Washington's administration brewing was encouraged by the federal government as an aid to morality. John Madison expressed the hope that the influence of brewing would extend to every state in the Union. A few years later Thomas Jefferson said, "No nation is sober when the dearness of fermented drinks substitutes ardent spirits as a common beverage."

A great wave of emigration started from Germany to the United States in 1846. These Germans who came to escape oppression brought with them a demand for lager beer, a light beer which became so popular among Americans that it almost drove out the heavier ales and porters. Brewing made big gains during the Civil War when excessive taxes were laid on the distilleries. The brewers did not suffer so heavily from taxation and so were enabled to increase their prosperity steadily until the passage of the Volstead Act.

As America grew in size and wealth beer became of increasing importance. Industrialization, with the monotony of a life in which the initiative of the individual vanished with the increased use of machinery, made the workman seek relief among his fellows in the saloon. The well regulated saloon was the poor man's club, the one place where he could alleviate his lot with beer and feel himself as good as the next man. Beer kept him content, and when a group of theorists, who may have had the best of intentions, removed the source of his contentment they started trouble that has cursed us with bootleggers, racketeers, contempt for authority and stomach ulcers.

We have become a devitalized people or we would have struggled to retain our beer. Imagine what would happen in England or Germany if someone tried to prohibit beer. The populace would assert themselves in such a way that the proponents of the idea would be lucky to escape with whole skins. In those countries they take their beer seriously and politicians are wiser than to meddle with it.

It should be illuminating to consider a few statistics on the consumption of beer in the United States. In 1840, when the first figures were available, the annual consumption per capita was 2.52 gallons of spirits, .29 gallons of wire, and 1.36 gallons of beer. By 1860 the figures had changed to spirits, 2.86 gallons; wine, .34 gallons, and beer, 3.22 gallons. At the beginning of the present century the use of beer had grown enormously while there had been a considerable decrease in the volume of spirits which the people drank. The figures for 1900 are: spirits, 1.28 gallons; wine, .39 gallons; beer, 16.06 gallons.

The peak of beer consumption was reached in 1910 when the consumption per person reached 19.77 gallons. In 1918 the rate for beer was 14.87 gallons, but that for spirits had hit a new low of .85 gallons, the falling off from previous years being incidental to restrictions imposed by the war. Then came prohibition, and since that "experiment noble in purpose," such statistics as have been compiled, or estimated, are startling in their significance. Two estimates were prepared in 1930, one by the *Prohibition Bureau* which places the per capita consumption of beer at a little under 6 gallons, and another by the *Association Against the Prohibition Amendment* which says the figure is 6½ gallons. However, the last named organization avers that in 1930 the amount of spirits used was 200,000,000 gallons, or 1.65 gallons for every man, woman and child in the nation, which is the highest point reached since 1870. This, mind you, under prohibition!

One might compare the beer consumption of the United States with that of other places. Just before the war, when we drank about 19 gallons per person, England consumed around 28 gallons and Germany 27 gallons. The rate varied in different sections of Germany. The average for the state of Bavaria was 50 gallons per capita per year, while in Munich it soared to 70 gallons. Belgium, where considerable wine is drunk, had a rate of 47.7 gallons.

What do all these figures mean? First of all that prohibition in our country has done harm in increasing the amount of hard liquor drunk and decreasing that of beer, thus halting the trend towards real temperance that was making headway during the first eighteen years of the twentieth century. They also show that in countries where personal liberty is still in favor, beer as a potable drink leads all others in the amount consumed. Further, and this is most important, prohibition has not stopped the drinking of alcoholic beverages but in general has thrown the emphasis from the mild and nutritious beers and ales onto the less desirable hard liquors. The booticians who have become such prominent and influential members of our society have not pushed the sale of beers; they are interested in big profits, which can only be made from the distribution of distilled products. In addition, many persons who had acquired a craving for "kick" in their drinks preferred, when making liquor in their homes, to set up a still instead of a brewery. The distillates went further in their pathologic effect, but aesthetically much has been lost by the apparent trend from beer.

Beer is an even greater social factor in the life of the Germans than it is in that of the English. The universities have their drinking clubs and student corps where *"hochs!"* and *"prosits!"* resound to the clink of lifted steins brought together in salute. The Germans are a philosophic people, and beer is the drink of philosophers. It inspires conversation and discussion without vituperative argument. Is it any wonder that to the Germans the *Braümeister* is an honored dignitary and that the citizens love their *braü* houses and beer gardens? Sedate crowds of Germans will sit for hours around little tables and drink countless seidels of Münchner, Pilsner and other famous brews. They talk earnestly on weighty matters or listen to sentimental music, then go home in as orderly a fashion as when they arrived. The German is never so amiable as when he is humanized by the beer that is a certain solvent of rancor and churlishness.

Before prohibition, American youth, particularly in the colleges, was wont to indulge its gregariousness around a barrel of lager that fostered friendship and was conducive to comparative sobriety. Since the Volstead Act was passed spurious and often poisonous hard liquors have supplanted beer as the drink of young and old alike. The beer drinkers had simple tastes. They found a meaning in life that is beyond the ken of young Americans today. They did not need an accelerated tempo brought about by artificial stimulation in excess of reasonable requirements.

Sociologists are concerned over the present trend of morals and manners in the United States. They deplore the behavior of modern youth, its abandonment of the old standards, its disrespect, and its neglect of the amenities. The Eighteenth Amendment and its subsequent enforcement act are responsible for these conditions. We allowed our beer to be taken away from us without protest and when we realized what had happened we expressed our sense of outrage by flouting the Constitution and drinking everything we could lay our hands on. The niceties of social intercourse are as extinct as the great auk. Twenty years ago the phrase "to drink like a gentleman" had a meaning incomprehensible to the youth who has matured in the last decade. The suppositions that a man would want to drink without getting drunk, or that he could value liquor as a beverage and not as an intoxicant, are so old-fashioned as to seem ridiculous.

Our one consolation is that we have it in our power to end these malodorous conditions even though our misrepresentatives in Congress dodge the prohibition issue forever. All we need do is to cease our chemical experiments with synthetic gins and whiskies and resume the home manufacture and drinking of pure malt brews.

We of *The Company of Amateur Brewers* must lead the way! Our mission is not alone a pleasant one, but through precept and the dessemination of proper knowledge of the brewer's art we can help the regeneration of our errant brethren. Beer, carefully brewed in the home from the best procurable ingredients and after recipes that assure quality, will keep folk in the house o' nights, promote domestic tranquility, restore respect for the law, encourage sociability and good manners, and be a blessing to our people. Brothers, ours is a great and beneficient work. *Prosit!*

❧ THE DRINKS & DRINKING CUSTOMS OF OLD NEW ENGLAND. An Address before the Special Meeting, October 15, 1931. By Richard S. Cantwell, Guest-lecturer from the E. A. B. C.

Ah, well, my friend, I have seen many a pleasant party round a table, but never round a pump. —ANON.

GENTLEMEN: Tonight I am taking the liberty to talk to you about a subject that is not concerned strictly with brewing. I want to say a few words about the drinks of old New England. There is much that is interesting and amusing in the drinking habits of our forefathers, and some of their foreign recipes could well be tried in our less serious moments. If you are not familiar with kill-devil, flip, sack-posset, switchel, scotchem or whistle-belly-vengeance, you may enjoy hearing about them. If what I have to tell you is pleasing, I hope you will forgive me for not trying to increase your knowledge of brewing beer.

Shakespeare's phrase, "potent in potting" could be applied to the early American colonists. At first they were unable to raise barley and hops. There was also a dearth of skilled brewers. Whenever a ship arrived, the men flocked aboard to drink of the malt liquors they missed so sorely. Of course a certain amount of beer and spirits were imported but they were hardly sufficient to supply the enormous demand. The founding fathers drank water with reluctance and when they finally accustomed themselves to it, they boasted of the amazing fact that they could stomach it. In his NEW ENGLAND PROSPECTS, Wood voices the general opinion when he says, "I dare not prefer it (water) before good Beere as some have done, but any man would choose it before Bad Beere, Wheay, or Buttermilk."

It was not long before competent brew-masters began to arrive and barley and hops were grown in quantities that could supply the infant brewing industry just then started. The Virginians had learned to make ale from Indian Corn in 1620, and similar beer was made in Massachusetts. However, the people of The Old Dominion must have been slower in developing brewing than were the inhabitants of New England, for John Hammond wrote in 1656:

> "Beare is in some places constantly drunken, in other places nothing but Water or Milk, and Water or Beverige; and that is where the good wives (if I may so call them) are negligent and idle; for it is not want of Corn to make Malt with, for the Country affords enough, but because they are slothful and careless; and I hope this Item will shame them out of these humors; that they will be judged by their drinke, what kind of Housewives they are."

The Dutch in New Amsterdam seem to have been more progressive than their English neighbors for they grew barley and hops prior to such growth in New England. This allowed the patroons to do a profitable business selling malt to the settlements east of the Hudson.

Laws were passed to encourage brewing, and it was not long before further legislation had to be enacted to control the manufacture of ale and beer. The Puritans were not above substituting molasses or sugar for malt and otherwise adulterating their brews. This practise naturally enraged the ultimate consumers and severe penalties were inflicted on brewers guilty of such behavior. Brewing was thought of such worth to the community that President Dunster of Harvard College wrote the court that the brewing and sale of beer by "Sister Bradish" should be "encouraged and countenanced" as "she doth vend such comfortable penniworths for the relief of all that send unto her as elsewhere they can seldom meet with." Beer was the choice drink of the colonist when they landed and was always foremost in their favor.

We have all heard of the notorious "Merrymount Revels" which incensed the godly. The unrighteous who danced around the May Pole were animated by metheglin which they drank up under the term "leakage" from two hogsheads brought by the ship *Friendship* for delivery at Plymouth. The hogsheads were tapped at Boston, consequently only six gallons of the liquor reached its destination. The colonists also made their own metheglin of fermented honey, herbs and water. This drink was common to the ancient Britons and the Picts who lived in the heather-covered hills of Scotland. In certain remote sections of America it retained its popularity until the last few years.

Apples grew abundantly in New England, and in the melancholy period when the colonists lacked beer they turned to cider. Every farm had its cider press and cider was a beverage enjoyed by children and adults alike. Before presses came into use about 1650 the apples were crushed by means of a heavy maul suspended from a spring board and striking in the recess of a hollowed log. Still earlier the fruit was pounded in a wooden mortar and the pulp pressed in baskets. The fact that in Massachusetts forty familes made three thousand barrels of cider in a single year and that ministers often needed forty barrels of cider to last them through the winter gives some idea of its consumption.

Hard cider was as much appreciated aforetime as it is today. It was drunk on every possible occasion. No christening, wedding, funeral, court session, town meeting, ordaining, training day, or notable event, was a success unless there was plenty of "cyder" and other heady drinks. In Vermont, especially in the Connecticut river valley, sheep farming prospered as it did nowhere else in the colonies. When the sheep were gathered for shearing housewives prepared huge accumulations of food, and after the wool had been clipped the assembled farmers sat down to feast, imbibe deeply of the plentiful potations, and enjoy a merited holiday.

Apple-jack was an early by-product of cider. The New England farmers made this strong liquor just as freely as they do now. We have all had apple-jack served in different ways from straight, to a complete disguise in cocktails. No matter how well it is hidden "Jersey lightning" always asserts itself. There is no temporizing with it. It is a direct, forthright drink that can not be ignored. Imagine the hardihood of a man who could down apple-jack, boiling water and ground mustard! That, gentlemen, is a drink for supermen, but in the good old days it was known as Scotchem—and for my part I feel sure it did.

There were numerous mild drinks that had some adherents. Cider-kin or water-cider was made by pouring water over solid dregs left after cider had been pressed from the pulp. At times it was flavored with molasses and ginger. Beverige was made in various ways; in some places with cider, spices and water; in other localities with water, molasses and ginger; and at seaports with vinegar and water. Switchel was beverige strengthened by the addition of rum. Ebulum (the juice of elder and juniper berries spiced and sweetened); perry (made from pears) and peachy (made from peaches) were other common drinks.

Our ancestors must have had stomachs of wonderful stamina to permit them to take the fearful drinks that they relished. For instance there was whistle-belly-vengeance. The name is enough to indicate that it was a drink of surprising potentialities. Sour beer was simmered in a kettle and sweetened with molasses. Crumbs of browned corn bread were then added and it was drunk as hot as could be borne. If that was not a test of the digestive organs it would be hard to say what would be.

Rum was at first imported from Barbadoes and went by many names. Kill-devil, rumbowling, ahcoobee and ockuby are a few of these appellations. Kill-devil was the term most usually used. West Indian rum was superior to that which was eventually made in and around Boston. The local product, called New England rum to distinguish it from the imported liquor, was manufactured from molasses brought into the country by newly established shipping firms that soon grew rich on the profits of the trade. So much rum was consumed that President John Adams, who drank a quart of hard cider before breakfast every day until he died, remarked that "if the ancients drank wine as our people drink rum and cider, it is no wonder we hear of so many possessed of devils."

Rum was so well thought of that in the Revolution both armies bought it by the thousands of gallons. It was deemed so essential to the troops that John Hancock wrote Major-General Lincoln on August 15, 1781:

> "As to *Rum* there has been a quantity procur'd and sent to Springfield and we have lately been affording assistance to the *Qu. Mr. Genl.* to enable him to transport it to *Camp.* It is of such importance that the army should be fill'd up and regularly supplied, that you may depend no *Exertions* of the *Executive* here shall be wanting to affect those purposes."

Black-strap was a composition of rum and molasses that stood in casks in all stores and taverns. Wily storekeepers and publicans hung a salted codfish beside the barrel to arouse the thirst of customers and increase the sale of the refreshment. Rumbooze and Rumfustian, strangely enough, did not contain any rum. The first was made of eggs, ale, wine and sugar; and the last consisted of a quart of strong beer, a bottle of sherry, half a pint of gin, the yolks of a dozen eggs, orange peel, nutmegs, spices and sugar.

Rum and loaf-sugar were combined to make mimbo or mim.

The making of flip was attended by considerable ceremony. It was probably the most beloved of all New England drinks and was extolled by its admirers. The flip-maker took a quart pewter mug and filled it two-thirds full of strong beer. He then added sugar according to his taste and followed it with a gill of rum. In the meanwhile he had been heating the loggerhead, an instrument shaped like a poker, until it was red-hot. When the loggerhead was heated to the right temperature he thrust it into the mug of liquor. The contents of the mug immediately hissed, bubbled and foamed and became flip. Connoisseurs of flip delighted in the bitter, burnt taste given the drink by the hot loggerhead. Another type of flip had four spoonfuls of a mixture made from a pint of cream, four eggs, and four pounds of sugar, added to it just before putting in the rum and inserting the loggerhead. Bellows-top was flip caused to froth abnormally by beating a fresh egg into it.

The most widely praised flip, known from coast to coast, was that made at Abbott's Tavern in Holden, Massachusetts. Holden was on the stage-coach route from Keene, New Hampshire, to Worcester, so many travellers stopped at Abbott's and spread the fame of the flip far and wide. The recipe for the most important ingredient, a special beer brewed by the Abbotts, is lost; but a descendent of this historic inn-keeping family, John Phelps, of Northfield, Massachusetts, still knows how the flip was made.

Abbott's Flip

"Break three eggs in a quart flip mug and add a teaspoonful of sugar for each egg. Stir the eggs and the sugar together, then add a jigger (small whiskey glass) of old Medford rum and a jigger of brandy. Beat the eggs briskly while pouring in the liquor. Now fill the mug with beer. The loggerhead should be red hot, and when the mug is filled it is thrust into the liquid. The foaming, hissing result is Abbott's flip."

One-Yard-of-Flannel was also a variety of flip made as follows: ale was brought almost to the boil in one pitcher while in another four eggs were beaten up with four ounces of moist sugar, a teaspoonful of grated nutmeg or ginger crushed in a mortar with dried lemon peel, and a quarter of a gill of rum. When the ale was heated the contents of the two pitchers were poured back and forth from one to the other until the mixture was smooth as cream. The loggerhead, also called flip-dog or hottle, was then thrust in as usual.

Punch, from the Hindustani *panch,* was also in heavy demand by tipplers. *Panch* means five, and refers to the number of ingredients in the original drink as it was made in India. Punch was the polite drink at social gatherings and was esteemed in all the colonies. There were any number of ways in which punch was made and almost everyone had his favorite recipe. The East Indians used only tea, water, sugar, lemons and arrack, but in the course of time its different makers used nearly every liquor available and all the tropical fruits they could get. It has suffered remarkable changes in the course of years but is still the mainstay of large parties. The subject of punch is too exhaustive for me to treat at greater length, but I suspect that each of you know many ways of making it that please you. If you would like more recipes you can refer to any cook book published before prohibition.

I want to impress on you what expert topers these old New Englanders were. They did not believe in half measures when it came to drinking. For instance, at a dinner in Boston in 1792, eighty diners drank one hundred and thirty-six bowls of punch, twenty-one bottles of sherry and a large amount of cider and brandy. Nothing is said as to the condition of these convivial souls when they went home, but how they could stay sober enough to move after having partaken of liquor in such quantities will ever remain a mystery. Yet this was not at all an unusual feat. I could cite plenty of instances even more indicative of an astonishing capacity.

Sack was a special make of dry, light-colored wine akin to sherry. By the eighteenth century the name was applied to all wines of the sherry class to distinguish them from Rhine wines and red wines. Sack-posset was the drink in greatest favor at weddings. The NEW YORK GAZETTE of February 13, 1774, printed:

"A Receipt for all young Ladies that are going to be Married. To make a

Sack-Posset

From famed Barbadoes on the Western Main
Fetch sugar half a pound; fetch sack from Spain
A pint; and from the Eastern Indian Coast
Nutmeg, the glory of our Northern toast.
O'er flaming coals together let them heat
Till the all-conquering sack dissolves the sweet.
O'er such another fire set eggs, twice ten,
New born from crowing cock and speckled hen;
Stir them with steady hand, and conscience pricking
To see the untimely fate of twenty chicken.
From shining shelf take down your brazen skillet,
A quart of milk from gentle cow will fill it.
When boiled and cooked, put milk and sack to egg,
Unite them firmly like the triple League.
Then covered close, together let them dwell
Till Miss twice sings: You must not kiss and tell.
Each lad and lass snatch up the murdering spoon,
And fall on fiercely like a starved dragoon."

Sweet wines were those in most demand. Canary, palm wine, tent wine, malaga, vendredi, passados, madeira and alcant are mentioned in old records. Brandy and sherry were also imported, and excellent native wines were made from cherries, peaches, blackberries, wild grapes, dandelions and elderberries. Spiced and mulled wines were always ready at every tavern and were served frequently in the homes. Everyone tried to be a poet, and as a result recipes were often written in rhyme. Here is one:

Mulled Wine

First, my dear madam, you must take
Nine eggs, which carefully you'll break;
Into a bowl you'll drop the white,
The yolks into another by it.
Let Betsy beat the whites with a switch,
Till they appear quite froth'd and rich.
Another hand the yolks must beat
With sugar, which will make them sweet;
Three or four spoonfuls maybe'll do,
Though some, perhaps, would take but two.
Into a skillet next you'll pour
A bottle of good wine, or more;
Put half a pint of water, too,
Or it may prove too strong for you:
And while the eggs by two are beating,
The wine and water may be heating;
But when it comes to boiling heat,
The yolks and whites together beat.
With half a pint of water more—
Mixing them well—then gently pour

> *Into the skillet with the wine,*
> *And stir it briskly all the time.*
> *Then pour it off into a pitcher;*
> *Grate nutmeg in to make it richer;*
> *Then drink it hot, for he's a fool*
> *Who lets such precious liquor cool.*

Negus was a warm wine punch invented by a Colonel Negus in the reign of Queen Anne. To the juice of a lemon the thinly cut peel was added with a bottle of wine, sugar to taste, and boiling water according to the strength desired. Nutmeg was then grated on the top.

Sangaree or sherry cobbler was made with half a pint of brown sherry, two tablespoonfuls of sugar, a slice of pineapple and pounded ice. As in many colonial drinks, nutmeg was sprinkled over the top. When port wine was used instead of sherry the drink was called port cobbler.

Instructions for making sillabub are given in the following quaint wording:

Sillabub

"Fill your Sillabub Pot with Syder (for that is best for a Sillabub) and good store of Sugar and a little Nutmeg, stir it wel together, put in as much thick Cream by two or three spoonfuls at a time, as hard as you can as though you milke it in, then stir it together exceeding softly once about and let it stand for two hours at least."

Another sillabub consisted of the juice of two lemons, half a pound of sugar, mixed in a bowl, a pint of sherry and grated nutmeg. To this was added two quarts of milk.

Numerous settlers came from Scotland and Ireland. They had been used to making whiskies at home and started distilling almost as soon as they landed. Whisky was distilled from rye, wheat, barley, potatoes and Indian corn. The Scotch-Irish in the south were responsible for the fiery "corn liquor" that has always been made in the hills of Virginia, the Carolinas, Tennessee and Kentucky despite all the efforts of revenue agents and prohibition officers to find the stills and cut off the supply. The southern mountaineers have that independence and stubborness that makes them unable to understand that a paternal government has a right to regulate the making or drinking of liquor. They consider this a personal matter with which any interference is to be resisted to the best of their ability. If you doubt that they believe in direct action go up any hill road in the wilds of the Appalachians and see what happens when you disregard the warning to turn back that you are sure to get.

Drinking was an aid to the promotion of colonial trade. I mentioned that the demand for rum helped ship building and shipping because of the liquor and molasses brought from the West Indies. Rum was also a big factor in the slave trade. Vessels loaded with rum went to the coast of Africa and traded their cargo for slaves which were brought back and sold to the southern planters. Then, too, a brisk business was done with the Dutch around New York, first for malt and later for schnapps or Holland gin. As a result New England accumulated wealth that began to display itself in the building of fine houses, the buying of household silver in place of pewter, and a desire for show. In other words, liquor was doing its part in forwarding the art of living.

This has been a discursive talk. I have rambled on without sticking to any set outline, and possibly I have mixed up my notes so badly that I have spoken of many things that do not properly belong in this address. I have just found among my papers a number of notes I had no intention of bringing, but since they are here I think they are interesting enough to read you.

Drinking Customs

"The word 'cup' for a drink began with the Romans. Cups were pledged to favorite deities and finally men pledged each other, the first drinking of toasts. At banquets they drank three cups: one to quench thirst; another, for pleasure, and a third, as a libation to Jupiter. Huge cups were used to serve wine. The cup of Hercules from which Alexander the Great drank his fatal draught held four quarts. The size of Roman wine cups gave rise to the phrase 'to get into one's cups.' Hercules was said to have crossed the ocean in his cup and as he fortified himself against the elements with wine became 'half seas over' in every sense.

" 'Bumper' is ascribed to the French *'bon pére,'* or good companion.

"The Romans hung pieces of ivy over wine-shop doors, as ivy was sacred to Bacchus. This occasioned the proverb 'Vendible wine needs no ivy hung up,' which has descended to us as 'If it be true, good wine needs no bush.'

" 'Boosy,' or 'bosky,' alludes to the shade of the bush under which the sleepy drinker liked to retire for a nap.

" 'Pegging away' is derived from the peg tankard which held two quarts of ale. Eight pegs were set in the tankard at equal distances, so that there was a half a pint of liquid between each peg. As a man drank he was 'a peg higher' or 'a peg lower.'

" 'Hob-nob' comes from the sociable habit of sitting around the 'hob,' or projecting corner of a fireplace, while drinking.

"When a Knight was about to depart for the wars or a crusade, or when he rode into his courtyard on his return, his lady came to his stirrup and served him a cup of liquor. Hence the term 'Stirrup Cup.'

"The 'Loving Cup,' was a capacious vessel of silver passed from hand to hand at ceremonious dinners. Each guest drank, wiped the edge of the cup with his napkin, and passed it to his neighbor. A more formal practice was for the person pledging with the loving cup to rise and bow to his neighbor, who, also standing, removed the cover with his right hand and held it while the other drank. This was a precaution to keep the right or dagger hand employed so that the drinker need not fear treachery.

" 'You may pay too dear for your whistle' and 'You may wet your whistle' originated in Scotland. A Dane who was noted for his powers of drinking challenged the Scotch to a match. The winner was to be the man who at the end of the bout could blow a silver whistle offered as the prize. A redoubtable Scotchman, Sir Robert Lawrie, won by imbibing for three days and nights and leaving all the rest of the competitors drunk beneath the table. Burns wrote of the memorable contest:

'I sing of a Whistle, a Whistle of worth;
I sing of a Whistle, the pride of the North,
Was brought to the Court of our good Scottish King,
And long with this Whistle all Scotland shall ring.'

" 'If you want any more you must whistle for it' came from the 'whistle tankard,' that had a whistle attached to it that was blown when it needed replenishing.

" 'Your health!' or 'Health be to you!' are from the 'waeshael' and, 'drinc-hael' of the Saxons. The bowls from which people drank healths became known as wassail bowls because of their connection with the old toast."

Now I will give you a little curious lore that may prove useful. It is from a book called VALUABLE SECRETS CONCERNING ARTS AND TRADES, published in 1795. This quaint and interesting work tells a number of methods by which to cure intoxication, as well as how to cause drunkeness without endangering the health. Some of the prescriptions seem a bit heroic, but our forefathers were not squeamish. Here are two ways to reform those "who are too much addicted to drink wine."

OLD SECRETS

1.

PUT in a sufficient quantity of wine three or four large eels, which leave there till quite dead. Give that wine to drink to the person you want to reform, and he or she will be so much disgusted of wine, that 'tho they formerly made much use of it, they will now have quite an aversion to it.

2.

CUT in the spring, a branch of vine, in the time when the sap ascends most strongly; and receive in a cup the liquor which runs from that branch. If you mix some of this liquor with wine, and give it to a man already drunk, he will never relish wine afterwards.

There are also given six ways "To prevent one from getting intoxicated with drinking."

TO PREVENT INTOXICATION

1.

TAKE white cabbage's, and four pomegranate's juices, two ounces of each, with one of vinegar. Boil all together for some time to the consistence of a syrup. Take one ounce of this before you are going to drink, and drink afterwards as much, and as long, as you please.

2.

EAT five or six bitter almonds fasting; this will have the same effect.

3.

IT is affirmed that if you eat mutton or goat's lungs roasted; cabbage, or any feed; or wormwood, it will absolutely prevent the bad effects which result from the excess of drinking.

4.

You may undoubtedly prevent the accidents resulting from hard drinking, if before dinner you eat, in salad, four or five tops of raw cabbages.

5.

Take some swallows' beaks, and burn them in a crucible. When perfectly calcined crush them on a stone, and put some of that powder in a glass of wine, and drink it. Whatever wine you may drink to excess afterwards, it will have no effect upon you. The whole body of the swallow, prepared in the same manner, will have the same effect.

6.

Pound in a mortar the leaves of a peach-tree, and squeeze the juice of them in a basin. Then, fasting, drink a full glass of that liquor, and take whatever excess of wine you will on that day, you will not be intoxicated.

If you want to get drunk without endangering your health—and who does not?—here is the method to use:

Infuse some aloe wood, which comes from India, in a glass of wine, and give it to drink. The person who drinks it will soon give signs of his intoxication.

Somehow there doesn't seem to be much fun in *that*. I think the customary method will be preferred even though you have a headache the next day. Another way, that I wouldn't recommend with any more enthusiasm, is:

Boil in water some mandrake's bark, to a perfect redness of the water in which it is a-boiling. Of that liquor, if you put in the wine, whoever drinks it will soon be drunk.

At last we come to information that in purpose, at least, we should all be eager to get. It is how "to recover a person from intoxication." Listen carefully, because you never know when you might need it.

> Make such a person drink a glass of vinegar, or some cabbage juice, otherwise give him some honey. You may likewise meet with success by giving the patient a glass of wine quite warm to drink, or a dish of strong coffee, without milk or sugar, adding to it a large teaspoonful of salt.

"To prevent the breath from smelling of wine." Ah! *There* is knowledge vital to all husbands who are suspected of undue conviviality! Just chew a root of *iris troglotida* (if you can find out what it is and where to get it) and you will be saved.

As a final thought to leave with you, I want to quote from an article which has a bit of appeal for both Drys and Wets, but which should interest all persons who believe in the middle path of sanity and temperance. It appeared in a Philadelphia paper on July 23, 1788, and here it is:

> A correspondent wishes that a monument could be erected in Union Green with the following inscription.

IN HONOUR OF
AMERICAN BEER AND CYDER.

It is hereby recorded for the information of strangers and posterity that 17,000 Assembled in this Green on the 4th of July 1788 to celebrate the establishment of the Constitution of the United States, and that they departed at an early hour without intoxication or a single quarrel. They drank nothing but Beer and Cyder. Learn, Reader, to prize these invaluable liquors and to consider them as the companions of those virtues which can alone render our country free and reputable.

Learn likewise to Despise
Spirituous Liquors as Anti-Federal

and to consider them as the companions of all those vices which are calculated to dishonor and enslave our country.

Gentlemen, you have been very patient with my feeble efforts. I have done my best to amuse you with the foibles of our ancestors. If I have failed the fault is mine. The fact that you have borne with me heartens me. Yours is a kind and courteous body, as one would expect enthusiastic lovers of beer to be. I thank you!

Wassail Song

Bring us in no brown bread, for that is made of bran,
Nor bring us in no white bread, for therein is no gain:
But bring us in good ale, and bring us in good ale;
For our blessed Lady's sake, bring us in good ale.

Bring us in no beef, for there is many bones,
But bring us in good ale, for that go'th down at once:
    And bring us in good ale.

Bring us in no bacon, for that is passing fat,
But bring us in good ale, and give us enough of that:
    And bring us in good ale.

Bring us in no mutton, for that is often lean,
Nor bring us in no tripes, for they be seldom clean:
    But bring us in good ale.

Bring us in no eggs, for there are many shells,
But bring us in good ale, and give us nothing else:
    And bring us in good ale.

Bring us in no butter, for therein are many hairs,
Nor bring us in no pig's flesh, for that will make us bears:
    But bring us in good ale.

Bring us in no puddings, for therein is all God's good,
Nor bring us in no venison, for that is not for our blood:
    But bring us in good ale.

Bring us in no capon's flesh, for that is often dear,
Nor bring us in no duck's flesh, for they slobber in the mere:
    But bring us in good ale, and bring us in good ale,
    For our blessed Lady's sake, bring us in good ale.

ANONYMOUS *(Tudor Period)*

❧ THE GENERAL PRINCIPLES OF MODERN DOMESTIC BREWING. An Address before the Monthly Meeting, November 1, 1931. By Joachim Behrens, M. D., Senior Warden of The Company of Amateur Brewers.

Qui non proficit deficit

ENTLEMAN, be seated. I appreciate your salutation, but I must tell you that I consider the welcome you have just demonstrated by rising, an honor to my office rather than to myself. This is a venerable and honored office, that of Senior Warden, and I assure you, my dear fellow members, that I shall always exert my best efforts to deserve it. And now to the subject of the evening.

There is such a yawning chasm between the large volume brewing of the olden time and the small volume brewing done today in our homes, that when it comes to speaking about the latter I fully realize that it is a most controversial subject. Everyone here has experimented widely and no doubt evolved theories from which beer suitable to private taste has come. But for the very reason that this subject is a fit one for discussion, I know you will be interested to learn that in examining the individual records of your experiments, I have come upon some general principles common to all.

It is about these principles that I propose to speak, for they are of importance to our new members and perhaps to others. Regardless of how many idiosyncrasies of the individual brewer have crept into the body of fact assembled in our archives, there is one main line of procedure which I find definitely sound. To consolidate these principles and put them into use is one of the great purposes of this organization. For it is only by the several contributions of each of you that *The Company* may justify its existence. So, gentlemen let me thank you now for the consideration you have shown me when I was obliged to examine, in perhaps a rather critical fashion, your special methods. If I tread on your toes in dismissing any of your pet discoveries, you may be sure that I have done so only in deference to the greatest good for the largest number. When I fail, on the other hand, to praise the many fine things I have found in the individual contributions to the archives, you may enjoy the consolation that comes through immersing your individuality in the glory of a common fame.

You have all used malt syrups and know the ways of making them into palatable beer. You know that malt is the basis of beer, and although many of you are probably learned in malting it may be well to say a few words about this difficult and involved process. I do not want to get into a maze of technicalities which would mean little to anyone but a chemist or a commercial brewer, so if what I say seems elementary to some of you I hope you will bear with me.

Malt and Malting

Malt used in beer is made from barley. There are two varieties of barley in general use—two-rowed barley and six-rowed barley. British beers are mainly made from the first mentioned variety, while in other countries six-rowed barley is the more usually employed. Two-rowed barleys are plumper than other kinds and have thinner husks.

The seeds of barley contain large quantities of starch, a stored-up insoluble food supply. Although the malt may contain as much starch as was in the raw grain it is converted into sugar, maltose and maltodextrins by the action of the enzyme diastase when the malt is mashed. These compounds, together with other insolubles such as proteins, are made soluble by enzymes during malting and are vital in that state for making beer.

In order that the enzymes may be formed and change the insoluble constituents of the grain into soluble forms it is necessary to start germination of the barley. It is equally as important to check this germination at a certain point. When the grain is brought to the malt house it is screened, dried, sweated, and stored until it is wanted for malting, when it is screened, graded, steeped, couched, floored, withered, dried, cured, dressed and polished, stored, and finally sent out as finished malt.

First the thoroughly cleaned grain is sweated by keeping it in a temperature of from 100° to 120° F. After this is done the barley is stored for some weeks before it is steeped.

The grain is next steeped by throwing it into cisterns filled to a certain height with water, the temperature being kept at 55°. The steeping period varies from forty-eight to seventy hours, according to the kind of barley. The water in the cisterns is changed two or three times during steeping, both to keep the grain fresh and to bring it into contact with the air so as to hasten germination. At the end of the steeping process the grain should have taken up about 60% of the water.

When steeping is finished the grain is taken from the cistern and made up in a pile called the "couch," in order that it can gather heat and start germinating. It remains in the couch for from twelve to twenty-four hours. Temperature and humidity conditions must be watched carefully. After the grain has been on this first or "young" floor for four days it should have begun to sprout. On the fifth day the barley is moved to another section of floor near the kilns or drying ovens, and is sprinkled. By the eighth day germination should have progressed considerably and the grain is spread thinly over another section of flooring. The barley is heaped up thicker and thicker by degrees while it is in a very moist condition, causing heating and sweating with additional growth of the rootlets. Production of sugar and the break-down of proteins now takes place. As the grain dries out and withers it is mellowed by enzymes.

When the endosperm or future stem of the green malt is soft and mealy and does not show moisture when pressed, but crumbles to a chalky mass, it is ready for the kiln. While in the kilns the temperature of the malt is slowly raised so that it is dried and cured. During the curing stage of kilning the malt must be turned frequently to assure uniform action. The final chemical changes are now taking place within the grain.

After the malt is cured it is heaped up for a few hours, removed from the kiln, and the rootlets are taken off. The malt is then stored in air-tight bins until it is wanted for distribution.

It is now pertinent to talk about the ingredients and general principles of modern brewing. Detailed instructions will be given you with each of our recipes, but there are processes and reactions common to making all beers.

Water

The first thing to consider is the water or "liquor." It should not be excessively hard. The chemical constituents of water do make a difference in the brew, but these are so slight that the amateur brewer need not worry. Rain water from wells or the kitchen tap will serve, although an eighteenth century housewive's manual says: "The best water, to speak in general, is River Water, such as is soft, and has partook of the Air and Sun. It is a Rule with a Friend of mine, that all Water which will mix with Soap is fit for Brewing." That may have been so at one time, but since the almost universal pollution of streams it would seem the better part of valor to ignore this advice.

Malt Syrup

The malt syrups which we purchase are made by grinding the finished malt, adding warm water, and making it into a mash. The mixture is then strained to remove all foreign particles and is boiled until it reaches the proper consistency, after which it is cooled and canned for the market.

Next we must take up the question of condition. Needless to say, it should be fresh. Crystalization or sugaring shows that the can has stood too long. Syrup is generally sold in cans of from two and one-half to three pounds, and the recipes used by our *Company* are based on cans of that size. A few ounces more or less will not make any difference in the final product. When you are about to use the syrup remove the paper wrapper and sterilize the can before you open it. This is necessary to prevent the introduction of germs in the water, for after you have poured the malt syrup into the liquor you should get all that remains in the can by rinsing it around in the water until it is quite clean. Dark malt is usually preferred, although whether your malt is light or dark will be largely a matter of personal choice as to color. Syrups range in price from forty-five cents to about eighty-five cents a can. The higher priced syrups are as a rule produced by former brewers and it is advisable to get them whenever possible. The increased cost of the more expensive syrups is more than compensated for by the better beer they make. You will also note that some cans bear the words "hop flavor." There is only one recipe we use for which this grade of syrup is appropriate, that for uncooked beer which we call *The Apartment Dweller's Special*. If, however, you wish an extra bitter hop taste, use the "hop-flavored" syrup with dry hops.

Sugar

There are two sorts of sugar that can be used, white granulated, and brown. If using brown sugar in place of white remember that you need twice as much of the former as of the latter. The proper sugar content of beer is of the utmost importance. There is a certain amount of sugar in the malt syrup, but the quantity that is added to the wort determines the strength of your beer. This applies to brewing in the home from malt syrup. Brewers who prepare their own malt do not add sugar, but rely on the saccharine content of the malt itself. The decomposition of the sugar in fermentation makes alcohol, and in order to keep brews of the same kind uniform you must be able to tell how much sugar they contain before they ferment. The general run of beers have from three to six per cent of alcohol. The saccharine content of the wort can be found by using a saccharometer, a variety of hydrometer showing the specific gravity of the mixture. This instrument has been called "the brewers' compass," because with it he can guide fermentation. Those of us who have studied physics will remember having used a hydrometer in laboratory work, and they should not find anything difficult about the saccharometer. Full directions come with each instrument.

Specific Gravity

"Original specific gravity" is the specific gravity of the wort before fermentation. Convention has made the specific gravity of the brewer one thousand times that of the physicist. A brewing gravity of 1050 would be expressed in physics as 1.050. As all beers contain a proportion of solids you can find out how much of them there is in your brew by dividing the excess gravity by 3.86. For instance, if the gravity is 1050 the excess gravity will be 50, and the solids content of the wort from which the beer is made is 50 + 3.86, or 12.91%. The solids or "extractives" are reduced appreciably in the finished brew.

Mild ales vary in specific gravity from about 1055 to 1072, with an alcoholic content of from 4.17% to 5.57% and a relatively large proportion of solids (5.7% to 7.3% in the finished beer). Light bitters and ales run from a gravity of 1038 to 1050, with from 3.81% to 4.61% of alcohol and from 3.2% to 4.1% of solids. The figures for so-called pale and stock ales are; gravity from 1059 to 1077, alcohol from 4.77% to 6.68%, and solids from 5.8% to 7.1.% Stouts and porters have a gravity of from 1054 to 1081, from 3.9% to 6.14% of alcohol, and from 4.5% to 8.8% of solids.

It must not be forgotten that the percentages of solids I have given you are those contained in the finished brew and will be found to be quite a bit higher in the original wort before the beer is strained. These extractives consist of malt sugar; various dextrins; substances between sugars and real dextrins; proteids and peptones holding nitrogen; phosphates; potash; and several other ingredients. Due to these solids, which are easily assimilated, beer has a high food value.

It is not practicable to go into a long and involved discussion of saccharometer readings. On the other hand you must bear in mind that to be a good brewer you should keep the different brews from any one recipe identical in alcoholic and solids content. This can be done by using the saccharometer to see that the specific gravity of the wort is identical in each batch of the same kind of beer.

In England Long's saccharometer is the one in general use. It shows how many pounds more an English barrel (36 gallons) of wort weighs than a barrel of pure water at 60° F. Balling's saccharometer is the standard instrument in America, Germany and Austria. It is graduated for a temperature of 17.5° C. and indicates the percentage by weight of dry, pure cane sugar in a sugar solution, or in a wort the percentage of dry extract the liquid contains. The graduations are marked by tenths from 0 to 20 or 25%, and a correction scale is furnished to allow for wort temperatures above or below 17.5° C. If, for example, the saccharometer sinks to the 12 mark it shows that 100 pounds of wort contains 12 pounds of dry extract of malt.

The saccharometer must be handled carefully. Clean it just before you use it. Hold it by the upper end and gradually lower it into the liquid, avoiding dipping it too deep. The liquid must be free from foam or gas and bubbles must not adhere to the sides of the saccharometer which must float free without touching the walls of the vessel containing the wort.

You can determine the alcoholic content of your beer after fermentation by the following method:

Find the specific gravity of your brew: then take a given quantity (100 c.c.) at 60° F. (15.5° C.) and evaporate it to one-half or less of its original volume. Do not let it boil during evaporation, unless you use a retort and condense the steam. The brew left after evaporation, or the distillate resulting if you employ a retort, is diluted with pure water to its original volume of 100 c.c. and the specific gravity is taken at the same temperature as before. If the gravity before evaporation was 0.9951, and the gravity after evaporation and the addition of water was 1.0081, .0081 shows the gravitating effect of dissolved solid matter in .9951 parts of original beer. In the gravity taken after evaporation all figures over 1.0000 show the extent to which dissolved solid matter affected the original specific gravity of the liquor. 0.0081 substracted from the original gravity of 0.9951 leaves 0.987, the specific gravity of the water and alcohol of the beer. By referring to the appended table of the strengths of diluted alcohols of different specific gravities you can discover the amount of alcohol in your beer. If the final gravity worked out to 0.987 the table would show your beer to contain about 9.6% of real alcohol by volume, which, parenthetically, is a great deal too much.

TABLE SHOWING ALCOHOLIC CONTENT OF LIQUOR AT
DIFFERENT SPECIFIC GRAVITIES AND A TEMPERATURE
OF 15.5° C. OR 60° F.

Specific Gravity	per cent alcohol by volume	per cent alcohol by weight	Grams of alcohol per 100 c.c.
1.000	0.000	0.000	0.000
0.99968	0.20	0.16	0.16
0.99937	0.40	0.32	0.32
0.99907	0.60	0.48	0.48
0.99877	0.80	0.64	0.64
0.99849	1.00	0.79	0.79
0.99819	1.20	0.95	0.95
0.99775	1.50	1.19	1.19
0.99701	2.00	1.59	1.59
0.99658	2.30	1.83	1.82
0.99600	2.70	2.15	2.14
0.99557	3.00	2.39	2.38
0.99515	3.30	2.64	2.62
0.99459	3.70	2.96	2.94
0.99417	4.00	3.20	3.18
0.99376	4.30	3.44	3.42
0.99322	4.70	3.76	3.74
0.99281	5.00	4.00	3.97
0.99241	5.30	4.24	4.21
0.99189	5.70	4.56	4.52
0.99149	6.00	4.80	4.76
0.99111	6.30	5.05	5.00
0.99059	6.70	5.37	5.32
0.99021	7.00	5.61	5.56
0.98984	7.30	5.86	5.80
0.98934	7.70	6.18	6.11
0.98897	8.00	6.42	6.35
0.98861	8.30	6.67	6.59
0.98813	8.70	6.99	6.91
0.98777	9.00	7.23	7.14
0.98742	9.30	7.48	7.38
0.98695	9.70	7.80	7.70
0.98660	10.00	8.04	7.93

It may seem that there is contradiction between the specific gravities and alcoholic percentages of the various types of beers and ales I have given you and those in the table. The explanation is that the gravities of the beers and ales are those of the brews when ready to drink, whereas the gravities in the table are those of the alcohol and water of the beer only, no extractives being present.

Determination of specific gravity and the use of the saccharometer are not so important in making beer from malt syrups as they are in the old-fashioned recipes where you do your own mashing. Malt syrups are fairly uniform when made by reputable manufacturers, and when used properly should always give about the same alcoholic content in each brew from the same recipe. When you do your own mashing you cannot employ too much care in checking specific gravities to assure uniformity of alcoholic content in the brews from different lots of malt.

Temperature

A thermometer is necessary also. Temperature must be correct, and the eye or hand can not give proper information on the amount of heat present. The temperature must be checked at all stages of brewing, and the words written by a brewer nearly a hundred years ago are equally pertinent today:

> The scientific brewer . . . knows and appreciates the value of these instruments; and to tell him to brew a certain quantity of ale from a given quantity of malt, without the aid of the thermometer and saccharometer, would be the same as to tell a captain to go to sea without his compass. Each would be at a loss how to proceed; and the issue to both, in all likelihood, would be complete failure.

Hops

Hops act on beer as a flavoring and a preservative. Before the introduction of hops spices were used instead. Hop-growing is carried on
throughout the temperate zones, but most of our hops come from New
York state and the west. The hop is a climbing plant and the fruit,
resembling a burr or catkin, is picked early in September. The hops
are dried and cured in a kiln or hop-house and are then baled for ship-
ment. When sold by malt-stores or groceries, hops come in half-pound
packages that retail for twenty-five cents each. The best hops are free
from mold, silky, bright, and straw-colored. When rubbed between
the hands a rich glutinous substance should be felt, with a fragrant
smell, and a fine yellow powder (lupulin) will appear. Lupulin is
the element in hops that makes them valuable in brewing. The best
color for hops is a fine olive-green, but if they are too green they have
been picked too soon and will lack flavor. If they are of a dusty brown
color they have been picked too late and should not be used. When a
year old they are said to lose one-fourth in strength.

Yeast

Fermentation is the aim of the whole brewing process and is brought
about by the use of yeast. The action of the enzymes in the yeast breaks
down the sugar in the wort and releases the alcohol it contains. Yeast
is a plant culture, a living organism, but there are so many complica-
tions connected with its cultivation and preparation for commercial use
it is not possible to discuss them for lack of space. The two main types
of beers—"top fermentation" and "bottom fermentation" beer—are
caused by different kinds of yeast. In making top fermentation beers
the yeast rises; in bottom fermentation beers it settles.

In the ordinary yeast cake, such as Fleischmann's or Red Star, the
yeast is mixed with flour. In this way it can stay alive for a few days.

Yeast used in brewing should be fresh. A stale yeast cake is hard, while a fresh one is soft and crumbly. Manufacturers deliver fresh yeast cakes to the stores at least twice a week, taking back those that are not sold. It is best to buy your yeast the same day you are to use it and keep it in a refrigerator until you are ready to put it in the wort.

You need not bother about Brewer's Yeast at this time. It is doubtful if you will ever want to make it, but as a matter of information you will probably be given a short description of its manufacture in some later address.

In common walks of life, cleanliness is next to godliness, but when it comes to brewing, the former* is the most important. Too much can not be said about the supreme necessity of having all tubs, crocks, barrels, funnels and coppers exceedingly clean. There are several diseases of beer which cause it to turn sour or become flat, and these diseases are caused by unfriendly bacteria. They can, however, be eliminated by sterilization. The capacity for taking infinite pains is to be applied to the noble art of beer-making as well as to other arts . . . and this capacity should be spent first and foremost in having all utensils as clean as boiling water will make them.

Brewers' Utensils

I want to speak briefly of the utensils that all expert small volume brewers should possess. It is evident from my survey that brewers' utensils *may* be of an infinite variety and often of strange sorts, for every man likes to surround himself with a lot of paraphernalia whether it be needed or not. However, there are certain things that are of a surpreme necessity and these I shall mention.

---

* When Dr. Behrens delivered this address, he definitly stated "the latter" at this point. But he later realized the error and asked the editor to correct it, with the statement that Dr. Behrens was slightly confused at the time.—EDITOR.

First you will need a boiler, unless you resort entirely to the one recipe for uncooked beer and none of us will do that I am sure. This boiler must be of solid copper. If put to it, a copper wash boiler is satisfactory, but I recommend what is known as a stock-pot used in restaurant kitchens to cook soup. This has a cover and may be purchased of mail order houses at a low cost, the price asked by Montgomery & Ward being only $2.89 for a six-gallon size. When it comes to you, it will be splotched with a dark greasy discoloration which you must take great care to remove by scouring long and thoroughly with hot water and bon-ami powder or some other cleanser, then rinsing many times with boiling water. The cover is important, as it must be kept on while boiling the wort, though you will need to punch a hole in the cone-shaped top of it or it will blow off. Wort cooking in this boiler gives off a strong but, withal, pleasing aroma which you may, if necessary, eliminate from the atmosphere by burning coffee in a tin dish.

After the wort is boiled it then goes into the fermenting vessel. For this I recommend a crock. Crocks come in six- and eight-gallon and larger sizes. I advise the eight-gallon size for brewing small volumes. The kind with folding-down handles is the best. Others use tubs, and between the two there is not much choice so far as the quality of the beer is concerned if they be kept equally clean; but the crock is more easily handled than the wooden tub and is also easier to clean. If you wish to try the tub, however, you can make it by sawing a cask in two, or by getting an empty butter firkin. Be sure to keep water always in the tub after you have brewed, as it should not be suffered to get dry. In breweries the wooden vats are varnished inside with shellac which insures cleanliness. Some prefer a fermenting tub made of wood with a spigot about three inches from the bottom by means of which you may draw off your wort into a funnel and then bottle directly.

Then comes the rubber siphoning tube. There are now tubes on the market which have a strainer at one end that floats and a shut-off at the other. There are others with a small cap at one end inside of which is a sponge for straining. I recommend the first kind, which should be of red rubber.

For bottling you will need a bottler and metal caps. The old notion of corking and tieing or wiring the corks down is too slow for the modern brewer and, after all, capping serves the same purpose with less trouble. When the beer is bottled it is best to set it on a cellar floor, but not in too cold a place, for the temperature should not be less than 40° F. Beer, of course must not be iced or too cold when consumed, but I find that if you will bring up your bottles about two hours before using and place them in a refrigerator the temperature will be about right. The average temperature of an electric refrigerator is near 45°, while that of the ice box is somewhat higher.

In the talks which you have heard, and are yet to hear, you may find more or less repetition. That is quite likely when different speakers without full knowledge of other speeches appear before you. But, if this is so, you can be consoled with the thought that important facts can not be too firmly impressed on the mind. I mention this because I am about to tell you something of an elementary nature about the successive steps in brewing. In later meetings detailed descriptions of how to make particular brews will probably amplify my brief statements.

We will assume that the actual heating of the liquor, adding of the malt syrup, salt and sugar, and the hops have been completed, and the beer is ready to be fermented. The wort is now strained and the yeast is added when the liquid has cooled to a lukewarm temperature.

Temperature

The temperature of the room where fermentation is to take place must be kept even. The true guide is the warmth of the wort, which absorbs heat generated by fermentation and should never get above 70°-75°. The room should therefore be cool enough to prevent higher temperatures in the wort. If the wort is too cool fermentation will be slowed up, while if it is too warm fermentation will be stimulated to an excessive degree, in which case the beer must be watched very carefully so that it can be bottled as soon as it stops working. It must be understood that the temperatures mentioned are for the average brew. Normally a room heated to from 50° to 60° will be ideal. Certain beers and ales need different temperatures to develop properties peculiar to them. The chief thing to remember is that regardless of time or temperature malt liquors must be bottled immediately when primary fermentation has stopped, but not until then. You must be eternally vigilant, as unforseen temperature changes or other causes may retard or accelerate fermentation and compel you to bottle your beer sooner or later than the recipe, which assumes average ideal conditions of brewing, tells you to. This is where there is no guide so sure as the instinct that you acquire with experience.

Yeast Head

Within a few hours after the yeast has been added, the beer starts to work and a scum rises to the top. This scum must be skimmed off each night, in most methods. The scum takes various shapes at different stages of fermentation. At first it is a light curley mass called "cauliflower" or "curly" head: as it becomes lighter and more solid it is known as "rocky" head; then it shrinks to a compact mass, the "yeasty" head. By the time the yeasty head has formed the sugars have broken down sufficiently to generate volumes of carbon dioxide which passes off in bubbles that escape with a continuous hissing sound. As the concentration of alcohol increases it has the effect of decreasing the vitality of the yeast until the point is reached where fermentation has apparently ceased. "Primary" fermentation is then finished and the beer is to be bottled for "secondary" fermentation.

Racking

The beer is now casked or bottled, a process known to the brewers as "racking." There are many ways of bottling beer. The main thing to remember is that the sediment in the bottom of the crock must not be stirred up. In fact the crock should not be moved or disturbed after the beer has started to work. If you plan to bottle by siphoning, set the crock on a bench or shelf before fermentation takes place in order to raise it above the level of the bottles. The easiest method of bottling is to siphon the beer from tub to bottle with a rubber tube. Be sure to keep the tub end of the tube near the surface to avoid stirring up the yeasty residue in the tub or crock. Clean the bottles thoroughly with boiling water before the beer is put into them. If you use a tub with a spigot about three inches from the bottom you can draw off the beer through a funnel and bottle directly from the spigot.

The best siphons are those previously described, with a built-in filter or a sponge strainer. Beer should always be strained or filtered at some stage of manufacture to remove the particles of solid matter that are not in solution. Beer filters or strainers can be bought from supply houses. The best kind, sold especially for cleaning beer cost about $12. Beer may also be bottled with a dipper and a funnel. Some prefer this method, and it is worth knowing about when a proper tube for siphoning is not at hand.

I have found statements in old books that to put beer in wet bottles will turn it mouldy and form mother, but I have never been able to prove this assertion. To be on the safe side, dry your bottles. When they are filled the beer should come within an inch of the top so as to have as little air as possible in the bottles.

When the beer is in the bottles—and five gallons of beer will fill about forty-eight bottles—it is ready for capping. You can buy tools for capping, but however you do it be sure that every cap goes on firmly. If a cap fits easily the bottle is probably smaller than standard size. Small necked bottles, or those with chipped rims, should be thrown away, as it is usually impossible to cap them so that they are air tight. Never use caps a second time for the same reason.

The bottles should be stored upright in a cool place until they are wanted for use. If the beer has been fined with isinglass there will be little residue in the bottom of the bottles, but if it was not fined you can avoid stirring up the yeasty sediment by careful pouring. When a bottle is emptied, fill it with water at once. If this is done the sediment is removed with ease and labor is saved when you wash the bottles.

Sugar in Bottles

Some recipes call for a half or a quarter of a teaspoonful of sugar to be placed in each empty bottle before it is filled with beer. This can be done best by means of an ingenious device known as a sugar-spacer. However, it is not adjustible and only measures half teaspoonfuls, so that it is impracticable where the recipe requires any other amount of sugar. You can then resort to measuring-spoons used in cooking and sold in any Woolworth's store for ten cents.

When the beer is first bottled it will be slightly cloudy, but as secondary fermentation progresses it will gradually clear. Although fermentation apparently ceases before bottling, it really goes on slowly afterwards until all the sugars have been converted into alcohols and carbon-dioxides. The carbon-dioxide gas cannot escape as it did during primary fermentation and this is the cause of the beer being lively. When completely clear the beer is ready for use.

Had the beer been exposed to air during the secondary fermentation it would have become sour and flat, due to the activities of acid-forming bacteria which break down the complex alcohol into acetic acid and water. Fortunately, this type of bacteria can thrive only when in contact with a plentiful supply of oxygen, so bottling after the primary fermentation prevents the bacteria from working in the beer. It is bacteria of this same sort that changes cider into vinegar if the barrel is left open after primary fermentation.

I think that is about all I have to say this evening. I have tried to be concise, but I have been dealing with a complicated subject that could only be covered fully by many books. There is so much technical matter connected with the biology, chemistry, and mechanics of beer and its ingredients—especially when considered scientifically and commercially—that it would be easy to become so involved that no one could get anything usable from what would be said. I hope those of you who are vastly learned will agree with me about this and bear with me for the sake of our newer bretheren who should not be confused by non-essentials.

❧ COMPANY RECIPES FOR MODERN DOMESTIC BREWING. An Address before the Monthly Meeting, November 1, 1931. By Major Ethan K. Stevens, D.S.M.

Medium tenuere beati

MEN OF THE COMPANY: Tonight it is my privilege as well as my pleasure to welcome the new members who have honored us by joining this society. I only wish they might have been present when on October 1, Dr. Wallace delivered his fine address on the purposes and aims of *The Company*. Nevertheless I can assure them that they will find a real fellowship among the brethren. Those of us who are more experienced in all that pertains to the craft of brewing (that fine craft we have banded together to perpetuate) will be happy, I am sure, to pass on our knowledge to others who may not have had such opportunities for extensive study.

Ben Johnson, that rare soul has said, "As he brews, so shall he drink." Thus we are led to say that since we are all somewhat familiar with the proper way of doing the latter, we ought to be equally familiar with the former. We want to do all we can to arouse a passion for the gentle art of both. This is not simply because we care much for the nectar of the vats and the several pleasures of its consumption, but also because we believe with heart and soul that brewing by the individual does foster a sturdy independence and that it makes craftsmen who can find relief from the drudgery of the machine age. Most of us are or have been victims of the monotonous routine engendered by this age. We do the same deadly things in the same deadly way, day after day. I use the word deadly advisedly, for actions not backed by a passionate interest or led forward by imagination are deadly to the soul of man. But if we adopt a craft as an avocation, and surely there is none more worthy or spiritually profitable than brewing, we shall find ourselves better men for having done so. We shall, I guarantee, recapture something of the vital interest in life that animated workers before they become slaves to machines and to "high-pressure" business.

Schiller, no doubt in a moment of ecstacy, said, *"Ich habe genossen das irdische Glück, ich habe gelebt und geliebet."* He must have realized that to taste the good earth one had to live and love with good spirit and with some gusto. I am sure you new members will find what the elder members already know—that in our gatherings and discussions there is a strong feeling of more than conviviality. There is a feeling of understanding, companionship and of the workings of a mutual imagination. All this cannot but stimulate you mentally. And the interchange of other ideas with kindred souls here will certainly stimulate you toward a realization that *The Company of Amateur Brewers* is a brotherhood for only men of the higher orders. After one of our meetings, your mind will be refreshed and you will be able on the morrow to tackle daily problems and daily labor with surprising energy and new zest. But, as no less an authority than the sainted Thomas à Kempis has said, "Tomorrow is uncertain, and how knowest thou that thou shall live till tomorrow?" How indeed? That is why our meetings are laid to make the most of the fleeting hours. That is why they are full not only of the companionship of kindred fellows but replete too with new knowledge which you will all relish.

I know that you who have made but little beer in the past will want to start brewing immediately. This is as it should be, for the sooner you begin, the sooner you will be adept.

You should not attempt the more difficult brews at first, for *pas à pas, on va bien loin* and may I add more surely and safely. The more difficult brews as concocted by our forefathers required a degree of skill that you can acquire only by serving an apprenticeship. Consequently I am going to give you tonight only such rules for the making of beer as I feel suitable for your initiation into the noble art of brewing.

Do not, however, stop with these. "Beware, froth is not beer," says the old Danish proverb. So do not stop with the simple approach to a deep and highly interesting subject. Go to the bottom of everything you do and make yourself sure as to the whys and wherefores for every step. By this method you will gain the most pleasure out of brewing, for verily it is no pleasure for men of parts blindly to follow instructions even though the results may be as good.

It has been supposed that brewing on a large scale is necessary to produce good malt liquor. This, however, appears to be an error; and though there are some difficulties in private brewing which are experienced in a less degree by manufacturers, yet there are some advantages in the former. Less heat is excited during the fermentation of small than of large quantities; and there is less danger of over attenuation, which renders the liquor liable to pass into acidity. When some of the fermentable matter is left unexhausted, it undergoes a slow and long-continued fermentation in the bottle, during which it mellows and becomes highly vinous. The great brewers, accordingly, have, in consequence, often fermented in small quantities; and chemists who have paid attention to the subject, farther state that malt liquors are best made in this manner in point of briskness, soundness, and body.

The Company Special

THIS RECIPE in my estimation is the finest ever put together for the small volume domestic brewer. It is the result of years of experiment. I have thoroughly tested it myself and no less than nine of you employ it in its essentials. It is simple yet produces the best beer that can be made from malt syrup in the home. Along with the instructions for this special brew you will hear many suggestions which will prove most helpful in all other brewing operations, no matter what recipes you use. So heed these things with open ears. The following materials are the required ones:

WATER	5 *gallons*
MALT SYRUP	1 *can*
HOPS	¼ *pound*
SUGAR	2 *pounds*
YEAST	1 *cake*
SALT	1 *level tablespoonful*

You begin by putting the water into the copper boiler and heating it to a temperature of about 100° or until lukewarm. Keep it over the fire and into it you pour the can of malt syrup. But first be careful to tear off the label and scald the can with boiling water. As you pour in the syrup slowly, keep stirring with a long spoon or ladle long enough to touch the bottom of the boiler and continue until all is dissolved. Then drop the can into the liquor and souse until all syrup therein is dissolved. This obviates leaving any syrup adhering to the bottom or sides of the can. At this point add your sugar, sifting it in slowly, then add the salt, stirring all the while.

You will in the meantime have broken up your hops and tied them rather loosely in a cheese cloth bag or in a piece of coarse cotton cloth drawn up and tied with a string. Now place the hops in the wort which by this time has become hot. Put on your cover tightly (be sure there is a hole in the top for steam to escape or you'll lose the cover) and wait for the wort to come to a sharp boil. When it does this, let it boil briskly for twenty to thirty minutes. If you boil longer it will do no harm but you must boil at top speed for twenty minutes at least. The important thing here is to have the cover on in order to keep in the sweet fumes and preserve the flavor.

If you cook the wort in the evening and then set it aside in the cellar or some cool place, it will be ready the next morning, for it is necessary to have this liquid come down to a temperature of about 100° or lukewarm to the touch. Some of you have pointed out a schedule which appeals to me. It is to do the cooking on Tuesday evening and set aside, completing the job on Wednesday so the wort is ready to bottle on Sunday. This should be much appreciated by those who save Sundays for pursuing this noble art.

Now, when the wort is lukewarm, squeeze all the water out of the hops in the bag and remove them. If by any chance the wort has become too cold, you can warm it by taking out two quarts, heating and pouring back again.

Now is the time for the straining and the yeast. Break the yeast cake and dissolve in a cup of warm water, stirring with a spoon. Up to now your wort is still in the copper boiler and the cover has not been removed since it was boiled. Set this boiler on a box or table. The wort must now be strained. Some do this with a plain siphon tube and through a flannel cloth stretched over the crock below. Another way is to have a siphon with a little sponge pushed into the opening at one end and a piece of pongee or shantung natural silk tied over this, siphoning with this end on the bottom of the boiler. I highly recommend the professional filter or strainer made especially for beer by supply houses. Now place the crock on the floor (be sure first to scald it) and let some of the wort run in. Add the teacupful of yeast solution to the wort in the crock and continue to siphon until it is all in there. Then place the crock on the table or box, tie a cloth over its top and leave. It is important that the yeast cake be fresh and do not forget to keep it in the refrigerator from the time it comes from the store until you use it. A day from store to brew is a safe maximum time.

If you make this beer in the winter in a very cool cellar you will need to cover the crock with blankets and warming cloths to keep the brew from falling to a temperature not favorable to fermentation. A room temperature of about 50°-60° is the best. A higher room temperature will cause quicker fermentation and this alters all time-specifications. This temperature of the fermention room is a very important point in all recipes. About twenty-four hours after the aforementioned operations have been completed the wort will begin to work and a deep foam will appear on the top. It is important in this recipe not to skim it off. Other recipes call for skimming off the foam. Great care must be taken not to disturb the crock in any way during the four-day fermentation period. Great care also must be taken during this time to keep the temperature even. If on one day your furnace fire goes out and the temperature in the cellar falls to 45°, or the next day it becomes so warm that the mercury rises to 80°, then all will be lost. The golden mean is a good rule in this process as in others. Try for a constant temperature of 55° and you will be safe.

About ninety-six hours after you have added the yeast and put the wort away to ferment, it will be ready for the bottle. Good brewers depend much upon the taste of the wort at different stages to apprize themselves of its proper progress. If you decide to pursue the art this far, begin by tasting of the malt syrup as it comes from the can, and then taste the wort each day. For the first two days and into the third day there will be the taste of malt and hops but on the third day as the foam goes away the wort will assume a bitter flavor. Do not worry. This is good and exactly what you want. On the last day the bitterness begins to vanish and this is the moment when you bottle. Just before the bottling stage the surface of the wort will support tiny spots of hop-resin resembling small bits of black dead leaf. These spots should be skimmed off.

Now we come to a most important element in this recipe. It is the placing of sugar in each bottle. Be sure your bottles are scalded clean and dried. Now into each small bottle (pint size) put exactly one quarter of a teaspoonful of white sugar. You can drop this in through a small dry funnel. Do not put in more or less but precisely this amount. Good brews have been ruined by too much sugar in the bottle. An over-abundance makes the beer foam too much and when you open it to serve there is too much carbonic gas. All this is bad but can be easily eliminated by care in measuring sugar. Get a quarter teaspoonful measure. Don't guess.

It is well to fill the bottles within one inch of the top. To cap a bottle no more than half full is a waste of both bottle and beer. It is also a safe indication that with too much air space at the top your beer will taste flat. When the beer is first bottled it is slightly cloudy but this will settle within a few days. Keep the bottles in a cool place. On the cellar bottom is a good one. The main trouble with most beer is this: people will not wait long enough for the secondary fermentation which takes place in the bottle. Everyone should wait at least a week before tapping the brew for drinking. Some will wait for two weeks but the real connoisseur who wishes to drink the beer at its best will want three weeks and then enjoy it. The foregoing then are the essential directions for making *The Company Special*.

Now let me tell you about some of the ramifications. A great many people object to the yeast sediment that will be found in every bottle. While it is possible to pour the beer without disturbing it, I will admit that the bottle would assume a much more professional aspect if the yeast could be removed. You can remove practically all of it by filtering with the beer filter referred to by Dr. Behrens. Others fine or filter their beer with isinglass. Go to the druggist and get two or three ounces of isinglass. There won't be a druggist in a hundred who know about this old and tried fining agent. Some will tell you to go to a hardware store as the assumption will be that you want mica. But you do not. Simply tell the gentleman that you want *Isinglass* listed as *Ichthyocolla* in the United States PHARMACOPOEIA for 1890 and in more recent editions of the British. Dissolve about one-third to one-half an ounce, in a quart of beer or wort. Let stand two or three days. Now add this to the wort the moment the fermentation is done just before bottling. By testing a bit of it in a glass of wort, you will see how long it takes for the isinglass solution to fine the beer.

Commercial brewers also used to fine their beers by "chipping." This consisted of adding maple or beech chips or shavings to the wort. The sediment adhered to the chips and allowed a clear brew to be drawn off.

It may be that you cannot bottle your beer on the fourth day after it has been put in the fermenting crock. On the fifth day the beer will acquire a flat taste. Do not let this make you despair, for you *can* save the brew. When you are bottling put one-half a teaspoonful of sugar in each bottle instead of the customary quarter of a teaspoonful. This is not good brewing practise under normal conditions, but is an emergency measure to save what would otherwise be a total loss. The beer will not be quite as fine as it would be if bottled in the usual way, but it can be drunk with considerable pleasure.

There is one more emergency to be considered. In very warm weather, when you have many visitors to your cellar, you will run short of beer. The week intervening between bottling and drinking seem a long and arid period. You will be appalled at the idea of being without cold, soothing beer for seven torrid days. You can avert this calamity by forcing a few bottles. When you start bottling, set aside some bottles and add half a teaspoonful of sugar to them. These are the bottles to be forced: keep them separated from the other bottles you intend to let stand a full week before using and in which you are putting the regular quarter-teaspoonful of sugar. The forced beer can be used the third day after bottling, and though it will not be as fine, it will prove as refreshing as a more seasoned brew. If the sun be hot and the throat be dry, you will find it good; in fact, very good. Cool to the temperature of a fine spring in the hill country and serve.

For your next attempt you might try

The North Country Special

WATER	5 *gallons*
SUGAR	2 *pounds*
SALT	1 *teaspoonful*
HOPS	¼ *pound*
MALT SYRUP	1 *can*
YEAST	1 *cake*

Boil 5 gallons of water in the copper boiler, then add the 2 pounds of sugar and a teaspoonful of salt, stirring the while. Now tie the hops loosely, after they have been broken up, in a cheese cloth bag and drop the bag in the boiling liquor. Allow the water containing the hops to boil for twenty minutes, then withdraw the hops and wring out of them all the water with which they are saturated. If the hops are not wrung out much of the hop flavor will be lost. At this point you add the contents of the can of malt syrup and continue boiling for another twenty minutes. Be sure the boiling goes on at a lively pace.

When the wort, as the liquor and malt syrup is called, has boiled the proper time it is to be poured into the crock or fermenting tub and set in a cool place with a temperature of about 50°. In the meanwhile, crumble the yeast cake into a cup of warm water and make it dissolve thoroughly by stirring it with a spoon. When the wort has fallen to a temperature of about 100°, or blood warmth, add this cup of yeast in solution and stir it into the contents of the crock. Now cover the crock with a piece of cloth to exclude dust and let it stand in the cellar or other place where the temperature averages 50°.

The wort will start working and a scum will arise which is to be skimmed off each night. An old-fashioned skimmer used by the farmer's wife to skim milk is a fine tool for this purpose. The wort should be allowed to work until fermentation stops, which is in about three days. When fermentation has ceased the top of the wort will be free from white yeast scum or foam. When the fermenting period is over the beer is ready to be bottled. Before filling the bottles put a quarter of a teaspoonful of sugar in each one.

You must be especially careful when siphoning or ladling the beer from the crock that the sediment at the bottom of the crock is not disturbed. If you think it desirable you can fine this beer with isinglass in the same way as in *The Company Special.* It is also practicable to clear the beer to a large extent by running it off with a siphon from the crock through a strainer made of flannel and into the boiler or some handy utensil that holds the full 5 gallons.

While it is possible to consume this brew after it has been bottled a week you would do well to curb your impatience and let it stand for two or three times that period. It is far better to schedule your brewing with a view to having sufficient quantities of well-seasoned beer always on hand than to be forced to drink new beer that has not stood long enough.

City people or those who have limited cooking facilities will delight in

The Apartment Dweller's Special

There are many of us, alas, on whom the exigencies of urban life in the twentieth century have worked hardships, or at least have restricted the freedom of our actions. Modern housing conditions and other disadvantages of city life bear down upon us on occasion. When you live in an apartment it is likely that you will not know your neighbor next door or across the hall, but you can be sure that he will have keen olfactory nerves with which he is certain to notice any unusual odors escaping from your kitchen. Although to you there may be joy and sweetness in the aroma of boiling wort, it is possible that there will be those to whom it is anything but delicious. You can avoid the black looks and muttered curses of these malcontents, if it seems they might complain too bitterly, by making your beer without cooking.

When conditions permit you to do so I recommend that you use cooked worts for your beer, following the recipe for *The North Country Special* or that for *The Company Special.* I do not want you to think the uncooked beer an inferior brew, for no beer is bad when it is carefully made of pure ingredients. It is entirely a matter of choice, and as the majority of people prefer the cooked beers to the uncooked variety it is natural to assume that most of you will feel the same way. In making beer without cooking the following materials are used:

WATER	5 *gallons*
MALT (HOP FLAVORED)	1 *can*
SALT	1 *level teaspoonful*
SUGAR	2½ *pounds*
YEAST	1 *cake*

Place 2 gallons of water in a kettle and boil it. A copper boiler is not necessary, since it is only the water that you need to heat. Put 3 gallons of cold water in the earthen crock or fermenting tub. When the first 2 gallons have come to a boil shut off the heat under them and add the can of malt, the sugar and the salt. While adding the ingredients to the water they should be stirred thoroughly. When you are sure that everything is dissolved, pour the boiling liquor from the kettle into the cold water in the crock, stirring it carefully until the mixture is at an even temperature. Now break up the yeast cake and drop it in the wort, cover the crock with a cloth, and set the brew aside to ferment. The room temperature during fermentation should be about 50°.

This beer does not need to be skimmed and requires no attention until the fourth day, when it is ready for bottling. Strain the wort through heavy flannel into another vessel, using great care not to disturb the sediment in the bottom of the crock. The utensil containing the strained beer should then be set on a box or table for siphoning off into the bottles. Before being filled with beer each bottle is to have a thimbleful of sugar placed in it. A miniature dipper of the proper size can be made by soldering a piece of wire to a housewife's thimble.

Let this beer stand for from five to seven days as a minimum before you partake of it. If you can allow it to rest for fourteen days it will be still better. Ingredients used in the amounts given in this recipe will make about forty-eight pint bottles of beer.

Liquid-Malt Beer

There are always those unfortunate souls who are pressed for time. The commuter dashes madly for the 7:45 in the morning and the 5:15 at night. He spends Saturday and Sunday tending his lawns and flowers, and week-day evenings he is too tired to do anything but go to a movie or play a little bridge. He is so continually on the jump he can not do things in a leisurely fashion even when he has the opportunity. Nothing seems as sinful to him as wasting precious moments. The world is full of these misguided or unlucky individuals who are constantly trying to save time in everything they do. They are found in all communities and in all walks of life. Hurrying, doing things in the shortest way, saving a minute here and a minute there, have become second nature to them.

Some men, of course, are victims of circumstance and are truly pressed for time, while with others habit and imagination cause them to act as though they were. Members of either of these two classes may like beer but feel that they can not afford to take the time requisite for the ordinary methods of brewing. These persons would hardly be members in full standing of *The Company of Amateur Brewers,* as it is needless to say we enjoy the process of making beer as well as drinking results of our labor. But we must be sympathetic towards those who have the taste for beer but find the longer ways of brewing inconvenient. For their sake I will mention another method of making beer which will not appeal to lovers of the craft spirit; but which may be used in case of emergency. It is the manufacture of beer from liquid malt.

Liquid malt is not to be confused with regular malt syrup. It is an entirely different product put on the market by several reputable brewing companies. The best I have examined and tested is made by the Cataract Brewing Company, in Rochester, New York. Beer from this brand has an authentic, bitter taste and is not overcharged with alcohol after fermentation. Other brewers in this part of the country, notably those of Troy, New York, make creditable liquid malt. It all comes in five-gallon square tins and sells for from $2 to $2.50. All the ingredients except the yeast are mixed in the liquid when you buy it. Some of the brewers furnish yeast with the tin as they deliver it, notably the Cataract Company, who recommend Red Star Yeast instead of Fleischmann's. Red Star used with Cataract requires two common-sized cakes. Fleischmann's, with other brands of liquid malt, needs only one cake.

Open the can of liquid malt with a can opener and put it on the stove over a medium fire. The malt is not to be made hot, but is only to be warmed. While the contents of the can are heating mix the yeast with a cup of warm water and put this solution into the crock or fermenting tub. Then pour the warm liquid malt on top of the yeast solution in the crock. Cover the crock with a cloth as usual and set the wort aside to ferment.

If the heat of the room where fermentation is taking place is 55°-70° the wort will need to stand for four days, but if the temperature is maintained at 70°-80° only three days will be necessary. If your brewing is to take three days, skim off the foam from the top of the wort on the second day and again the following morning. In the case of a four-day brew you do not skim on the second day but perform the operation on the third and fourth days. At the end of the fermenting period let the wort stand until you see it speckled with foam. Do not remove the foam, but proceed with bottling the beer. A word of caution is not amiss at this point. While I have said that fermentation should take three or four days, according to the temperature, you must be guided not by the length of time, but by the actual working of the beer. *Regardless of the time the Beer has stood in the crock do not bottle until all fermentation has stopped.* This applies not only to this recipe, but should be followed in connection with any brew you make. The customary procedure is to put a quarter of a teaspoonful of sugar in each bottle before adding the beer. Some brewers have found that they get better results when they do not use sugar, but bottle the beer without putting anything in the bottles. Try both methods and decide for yourself which you prefer. When it is bottled let the beer stand for seven days, and longer if possible, before you drink it.

Methods of Handling Beer

The methods of keeping and handling make a great difference in the quality and flavor of beer. Beers of the lager type are best when kept at about 40°. If for any reason the beer has become warmer than this it should be stored in a cool place, in a refrigerator if possible, until it has been brought to the proper temperature before serving.

If your beer is to be consumed from the keg and has not been bottled the first glass drawn from the keg should be thrown away. As soon as the beer ceases to run freely, a vent should be placed in the bung. If the keg is to stand for some time before it becomes empty a quantity of gas will escape every time the vent is opened. The beer will soon become stale and flat, and to prevent this a tube should be placed in the vent hole and be connected with a hand operated beer pump. The air pressure can then be regulated satisfactorily, but be sure that the pressure is not too great or you will draw off more foam than beer. It is necessary that the air supply be fresh or it will contaminate the beer.

Bottled beer should be kept in a cool place or in a refrigerator, but not against ice. Stand the bottles upright, for you want the sediment to settle to the bottom. Do not pour the last bit of beer from the bottle or it is possible that you will spoil your drink with the unpalatable dregs.

The beers you can make from the malt syrups and the liquid malts of the contemporary home-brewer are palatable and pleasing. If you brew them with the right degree of enthusiasm and loving attention to details they should reward you with the perfection of a golden liquid that does no violence to its devotees, but gentles and mellows the pot-tosser who partakes thereof. The bottles that you bring up from your cellar should be handled tenderly, and as you lift them to the light, admiring the amber glow within them, reflect on the innumerable generations of men who have found beer the most refreshing and desirable of all drinks. Approach the quaffing of beer with a certain humility, as of one participating in a rite, for beer of sorts was a sacred potation when the world was young. When the Druids burned their human sacrifices in wicker baskets, libations of beer were offered to the dark gods of the gloomy groves where they worshipped. Down the centuries beer has been a drink for the thoughtful man, the philosopher and dreamer. As you empty your bottle and the foam mounts in the stein, remember that you are about to partake of the body and blood of Sir John Barleycorn, that good knight who has become the patron saint of all true maltworms.

There are those among you who have visited Germany and know the fine body and flavor of the notable beers native to the country where malt liquor is preëminent as a beverage. You may have had the ales, beers, porters and stouts of England, and—heaven forbid!—it is possible that you were foolhardy enough to try the imitation beer the French make and disguise under the misleading title of "bock." Perhaps you have been to Scandanavia and in Copenhagen or Stockholm have dallied with the beautiful dark beers of Denmark and Sweden. If you have never been abroad, but are old enough to have visited, before prohibition, such noteworthy purveyors of gastronomic delicacies as Lüchows, the Hoffbraü, the Kaiserhoff and similar restaurants, it is unnecessary for you to go to Europe to learn about good beer. There was a day, incredible as it may seem in this era of bootleggery, when in New York and other cities of this country it was possible to get food that was prepared by artists of the saucepan and skillet, and liquors that were the rare and acclaimed vintages of the world. It was not needful to stir more than a few blocks from your own home to imbibe Bass's Ale, Guiness's Stout, or Haffenreffer. But if you were sensible you went to a German rathskellar where the solid, appetizing and filling *schnitzels, nockwursts, sauerbraten* and other dishes from beyond the Rhine were accompanied by dark Karlsberg, Münchener, Weihstefan or

Thomasbräu, Kulmbacher from Bavaria, Pilsner, or familiar Budweisser. Those were the days when dining was a fine art and restaurateurs vied with each other to please a discriminating clientele.

Today it is impossible to get the excellent brews that once delighted us unless we leave the confines of these benighted States. No longer can you descend into the subterranean depths of hostelries run by happy, hospitable, rotund Teutons and admire the enormous tuns that held the liquors dear to all who believed that drinking was an art. The young men, those who have reached their majority in the last ten years, can not understand that there was a time when a man could not be considered educated unless he knew the distinctive qualities of each brew or vintage, and the conditions under which it should be served. Drinking was a polite social accomplishment, not a preliminary to casting aside the conventions, and a gentleman was assumed to have a cultivated taste.

I suppose the statement that good beer is no longer obtainable in America might be qualified. There is still a haven for the thirsty that can satisfy the craving of the initiated. On the west bank of the Hudson river stands the old and largely Germanic city of Hoboken. For over a century it has had its beer gardens and *bier halles* to which connoissieurs of beer have made pilgrimages. The North German Lloyd boats dock along the water front, and the atmosphere of the town is much more like that of Hamburg than of New Jersey. Somehow the brews of the Fatherland filter through the cordon of agents who are supposed to intercept them. In Hoboken steins are still filled with honest beer and *geshundheits* are shouted as of old. If you have not reached the age when blessed memories of pre-prohibition evenings can be recalled, or find it impracticable to visit Hoboken or Europe, you can still know the joy of drinking admirable beer. All that is needed is for you to brew in your own home, following the recipes that I have given you. These recipes are all you need to initiate you into the glorious mysteries of brewing. They will permit you to have a goodly supply of beer in your cellar. Your less fortunate friends will praise your hospitality. They will help drink up the bottles you had expected to last some time. They will appear frequently, and enthusiastically. They will sing your praises aloud and afar. Your liquor may diminish, but your list of friends will grow amazingly. Of course you want friends! You want to keep those you've got, and you want to add new ones to your list. The fun—I won't use the word work, for that it should never be to a real devotee of Gambrinus—of constantly making new brews to replenish those that vanish down convivial throats, should fill you with gratitude to the appreciative consumers of your stock. Then, too, the oftener you have to brew, the more expert you will become. Instead of hurling maledictions at those who clamor for your last bottles, sympathize with them as did *Maitre* François Rabelais when he said:

"O the drinkers, those that are a-dry, O poor thirsty souls!"

❧ THE DOMESTIC BREWING OF THE OLDEN TIME. An Address before the Special Meeting, November 17, 1931. By Nathaniel Royce Bowden, M.D., F.R.H.S.

PISCATOR; *Come, hostess, dress it presently, and get us what other the house will afford, and give us some of your best barley wine, the good liquor that our honest forefathers did use to drink of; the drink which preserved their health, and made them live so long and do so many good deeds.*

—ISAAK WALTON

GENTLEMEN: It was gratifying to hear that our new brothers in *The Company* are so enthusiastic over the results of their brews made from the recipes given them at our last meeting. The talk by Major Stevens on Modern Recipes was for the purpose of showing you how easy it is to make good, palatable beer with simple ingredients, a few pieces of apparatus, and a minimum of bother and time. You are now embarked on a hobby that has infinite possibilties. There are any number of delightful brews of generations past that have much to recommend them. You will want to try them yourselves. Some of them are a little involved, while others are simplicity itself. To make them as they should be made you must adhere to the methods used before malt syrup, sugar, and all the modern conveniences simplified the work of the ardent home-brewer.

Until our next gathering, when Professor Rhodes will lecture on Old Time Recipes, I advise you to perfect your technique by continuing to make the beers you have already tried. You will develop an intuition for doing the right thing, and sensing trouble and averting it before it spoils your brew. The basic principles of brewing have always been the same, but in practice the ancient brewers used methods quite different from those with which you are familiar. I am going to tell you as briefly and clearly as I can what those methods were. Study them intently. It may be that you can modify them a trifle when you attain the rank of *Braümeister,* but without a thorough comprehension of what they were, you will be lost when you go to follow old recipes.

We will first consider the utensils of the old-time brewer. The average family brewed large quantities of beer at a time, and the vessels used were much larger than those to which you are accustomed. I will mention these utensils. They are based on a single brewing of three barrels of beer of eighteen gallons each.

Utensils

COPPER. A copper should hold forty gallons to allow for the hops and waste caused by evaporation during boiling. If a sloping sheet or collar of lead is fixed to the rim of the copper it will prevent the wort from spilling when boiling rapidly and return into the copper that which would be wasted otherwise.

GAUGE STICK. It is advisable to know the capacity of your copper when filled to any height. This is easily found by a gauge stick. Two gallons of water can be poured in the copper, the stick put in, and a mark made on the stick at the surface of the water. By adding a gallon of water at a time and marking the places on the stick where the surface comes after each gallon has been let into the copper, you will complete the gauge. The stick should be either black with white lines or white with black lines for ease in reading. Always gauge the copper in the same place, and this can be done if you mark a particular part of it as a guide. In the same way similar gauges should be made for the mash tub and the underback.

MASH TUB. The mash tub should hold sixty gallons, for this must contain both the malt and water, and permit stirring. It should be wider at the top than at the bottom, and the depth should not be quite so great as the diameter of the bottom. It would be well for your tub to have a false bottom of several pieces pierced with gimlet holes very close to each other. A hoop of wood two or three inches broad should be nailed around the inside of the tub, about three inches above the real bottom, as a support for the false bottom. A tap is then placed in the bottom of the tub so that the wort can be drawn off at the proper time.

MASHING STICK OR OAR. Two mashing sticks are needed. They are poles about six feet long, with a frame at the bottom across which there are six pieces of wood. The frame is twelve inches long, broader at the top than at the bottom, and shaped like an inverted shovel. Wooden rakes with long teeth will do equally well.

UNDERBACK. The underback is a shallow tub to go under the mash tub and receive the wort as it is drained off. It need only be one-half the capacity of the mash tub, but should have a greater diameter. A tap is fitted into the side.

COOLERS. There should be three or four coolers, rectangular pans the sides of which should be a few inches above the wort when they are filled to a depth of three or four inches. All coolers must be the same size.

TUN TUB. A tun tub of thirty gallons capacity is required as a receptacle in which the beer can work. The mash tub will serve as a tun tub for small beer.

CASKS. The casks ought to be bell-shaped, the narrow part at the bottom. A bung-hole at the top should be large enough to admit a person's hand and arm for the purpose of cleaning the cask. The bung-holes must be closed with wooden plugs that fit perfectly. You should have two sets of casks, in order that the second set may be filled when the first is tapped, that the beer may acquire age.

MEASURES. Use a good bowl or dipper with a handle and of exactly one gallon capacity as a measure.

FUNNEL. A wooden funnel is the best kind to use for filling the casks.

BUCKETS. You will need a couple of buckets holding about three gallons each.

SACCHAROMETER. This instrument is indispensable. Its necessity has been explained to you in the address on *The General Principles of Brewing*.

THERMOMETER. Buy a good Fahrenheit thermometer. When taking temperatures tie a string to the top of the thermometer and lower it into the liquid. Let the thermometer stay immersed for a minute or two, then raise the stem above the surface to observe the degree at which the mercury stands in the tube. Be careful not to withdraw the bulb from the liquid or the air will cool the mercury and prevent a correct reading.

A rare book on brewing gives the following advice about the care of brewing utensils:

" . . . be careful not to use soap or any greasy materials; a good brush and scalding water will generally thoroughly cleanse them, but all the fur on the sides or bottom must be removed; after this, they should be well drained, and left in some airy situation to sweeten. If they are still found to be tainted, take wood ashes, and boil them to a strong ley, which spread over the bottoms of the vessels scalding hot; then scrub with a brush or broom, or throw some stone lime into water in the vessel, and scrub over the bottom and sides, rinsing well with clean water. In some cases it is necessary to wash with oil of vitriol, diluted with seven or eight times its bulk of water. Fresh burnt charcoal can also be employed."

The Brewhouse

If you wish to emulate the gentlemen of the past and build your own brewhouse you will want to have a mental picture of what it should be like before you start construction. It should be lofty enough to let the copper be raised sufficiently high for the wort to run into the coolers, from the coolers into the tun (or fermenting) tub, and from the tun tub into the casks. The casks should be set on stands eighteen inches or two feet from the floor, which should be paved or made of cement. The copper should be placed near the entrance of the brewhouse and must be elevated higher than any of the other utensils. A ventilator above it will allow the steam to escape.

As near the copper as possible is the mashing tub. This will have a staging around it on which you may stand while mashing, and it must be far enough from the wall to permit free use of mashing-oar.

The underback is placed directly under the mash tub, on a temporary stand, high enough so that its contents can be drawn off into pails.

The coolers should be as near the mash tun as will leave sufficient space for the mashers to work freely. They should be at least seven feet from the ground and a little below the level of the bottom of the copper. They should be placed on opposite sides of the brewhouse, directly across from each other, and should be a little higher at one end than at the other, that they may completely empty themselves when the wort is drawn off. The pipes of the coolers are placed at the lower ends to conduct the wort into the fermenting tun.

Fermentation takes place in the tun-room, separated from the main part of the brewhouse by a wall. There should be a window admitting the north light and the cask-stands should be on the north side. The fermenting tuns should be separated from the ends of the coolers by the wall but be placed as near to them as possible, that the pipes may have easy communication from one vessel to the other.

The Ingredients

We can now turn to the ingredients you will use. The malt and yeast are in such different forms from those with which you are familiar that you will have to be given further information about them.

I want to say a few words about the water to be used. All of you know how important a part the liquor plays in determining the quality of the beer. Some of the chief differences between one kind of brew and another, usually geographically designated, lie in the liquor. In general the principle of selection is in this rule: soft water or water softened by exposure to the air, makes stronger extract and is more easily fermented, while hard water makes the beer that keeps the longest and seldom turns sour. Many soften water to be used in brewing by adding a spoonful of baking soda to a barrel; others employ a handful of common salt mixed with one ounce of salt of tartar. Most well water is very hard and should not be used except in an emergency, when it should be brought up and exposed to the air for some days before use. Rain water collected in a clean cistern is preferable to any other, being much softer.

Malt varies considerably in quality, consequently the amount of saccharine matter in wort made from a bushel of one lot of malt may be greater or less than that in wort made from a bushel taken from another lot of malt. The only guide to making your beer of proper strength is to know the original specific gravity of your wort and not rely on the amount of malt you have used to give you accurate results.

Use only the best quality of malt. Examine it to see that it has a round body, breaks soft, is full of flour, smells pleasantly, and has a thin skin. Chew some of it; if it is sweet and mellow it is good; if it is hard and steely, retaining something of its barley nature, it has not been properly malted. Another test is to throw malt in a glass of water. If the malt floats it is good, but if any sinks to the bottom it is not true malt.

The best malt is pale, the result of slow drying, and will produce more and better quality wort than malt that has been too much and too quickly dried. Amber colored malt produces a flavor admired in some localities. Brown malt loses a great deal of its nutritional value, but confers a distinctive taste on the beer for which it is used. Malt roasted after the manner of coffee is made from pale malt and is used to give the color and flavor to porter.

The malt must be ground to obtain the best infusion in the wort. It should be thoroughly crushed but not powdered. Each grain must be reduced, and grinding should be done from twenty-four to forty-eight hours before the malt is to be used. By having an interval between grinding and mashing, the heat engendered when the grain was crushed escapes and the malt mellows. It will also receive water better and a greater quantity of wort can be made than would be the case if the malt were used immediately after grinding. The malt is ground either between wooden or steel rollers, stones, or steel mills like coffee mills. Ground malt is called "grist," but becomes "goods" when put in the mash tub, and the extract is known as "wort." A bushel of good malt will, on an average, make one and a quarter bushels of grist. A "quarter," eight bushels, of malt will yield nine and a half to ten bushels when ground.

Mashing

You can now go ahead with mashing. Fill the copper with water and bring it to a boil. Ascertain the quality of your malt, as well as its strength, and having determined the amount you wish to brew, measure out your malt in accordance with the recipe you are using. Draw off the boiling water into the mash tun and add enough cold water to it to reduce the heat from 212° to exactly 182°. Any temperature above that will interfere with fermentation. When the water reaches the proper heat the crushed malt is to be thrown in and mixed with the water by constant stirring with the mashing-oars. This process will take at least twenty minutes, as the whole mash should be of equal consistency. The cover is now put upon the mash tun, sacks are placed over the top to retain the steam and heat, and the mash is left to stand for an hour and a half. If the wort is let stay too long in the mash tun it will be so cold as to lose transparency.

After the mash has stood the correct time in the mash tun the wort is run off into the underback, the tap being partially turned at first so that the pressure will not be too great and force out a portion of the grains with the wort. When in the underback the wort should have a fine transparent head, with a pearly froth several inches high. If the froth is tinged with red, and turbid, there was too much water at the time of mashing: if it comes down dead and without froth, the water did not have a high enough temperature.

During the hour and a half between running the first lot of water into the mash tub and drawing off the wort into the underback, the copper should be refilled with water to be boiled for a second extraction. The gauge stick will show you when nearly all the wort has run into the underback, upon which the second boiling of water, at a temperature of 190° to 195°, is let in on the comparatively dry grain by sparging.

Sparging

"Sparging" is sprinkling hot water over the mash at different times but at short intervals. This is done by running the water from the copper through a trough perforated with small holes at the bottom and sides, and hung over the mash tun. The trough should be capable of movement around every part of the mash tun. For the home-brewer who may work on a smaller scale, a two and a half gallon watering pot fitted with wooden handles to protect the hands from the heat will be satisfactory. If you begin sparging when two-thirds of the extract has been run off, the mash will be kept warmer, which is of great advantage.

After sparging has taken place, gauge the wort to see if you have the amount you want in the underback. You can count on boiling, the addition of hops, and evaporation during cooling, reducing the wort in the underback by about 35%. It will be necessary to draw off enough additional from the mash tun to meet this deficiency. When the required quantity has been run into the underback the tap of the mash tun is shut and a third boiling of water is cooled to 195° and run on to the bed of grains to make table beer. There will be enough wort remaining with the mash from the second mashing to make up the loss of 20% that will occur during the rest of the brewing process, so that the quantity of water should not much exceed the amount of beer intended to be made. Before all the water is drawn off the fire under the copper is damped and several pailfuls of wort must be poured into the copper immediately it is empty to prevent injury to it from standing dry over the fire. It is at this point that the wort is taken from the underback and put into the copper to boil.

Boiling With Hops

When the wort is transferred to the copper, one-half the hops are put in with it. The usual quantity of hops is a pound to a bushel of malt or eight pounds to the quarter. When this is well boiled with the wort for thirty or forty minutes the rest of the hops are added, thoroughly mixed, and boiled for half an hour. An hour is usually enough for boiling all the hops in the wort. Before drawing off the wort into the coolers, take out a portion and test the gravity with the saccharometer. The wort must be kept boiling rapidly, but when boiling is finished the fire is completely damped, and the wort is run off into a cooler through a large hair sieve in order to keep back the hops. To prevent the hops from subsiding to the bottom of the copper the wort should be stirred while it is running into the cooler.

Table Beer

In the meanwhile the second extraction, which is for table beer, should be drawn from the mash tub into the underback, ready to replace the wort being removed from the copper to the cooler. If there should not be enough table-beer wort, add as much cold water as is necessary to allow for the 30% or 35% it will probably have lost. This cold water will be poured over the grains the same as hot water and will extract any good remaining in the malt. Boil the table beer in the copper for an hour and a half, together with the strained boiled hops, as soon as the first extraction has been run off into the cooler.

Cooling

The wort should fill the cooler only to a depth of four or five inches so that it will cool quickly, especially in warm weather. Dense wort is particularly liable to injurious chemical changes when exposed to warm air. Wort should not be left in the cooler more than eight hours; nor should it be allowed to cool in less than three, as it should have this time to deposit its impurities in the cooler. After the wort is run off, the cooler will be found to be coated with slime that would communicate a disagreeable flavor to the ale if it were allowed to get into the fermenting tub. Regular coolers, such as I have described, have a big advantage over an odd assortment of vessels used to cool beer. If a number of assorted coolers are used there is loss in the separation of the wort, for some adheres to each vessel, and the sediment is disturbed when the wort is poured off, some of it going into the tun tub with the liquid. By cooling the wort in two coolers it can be removed at one degree of heat, an impossibility when the wort is at different depths in a variety of vessels. If the first quantity of wort poured into the tun tub is from a small vessel it will have a different temperature than the next lot taken from a larger container. Fermentation will be unduly hastened, the wort will be foxed, and the yeast will not separate itself.

Yeast

Before I take up the subject of fermentation I want to describe brewer's yeast. It is a solid, soft substance, grayish-yellow in color. It dries to a pale brownish mass nearly insoluble in water, and it readily putrefies when moistened. The best yeast is that thrown out of the bung-holes of casks. It deteriorates when kept unless it is pressed and all the liquid portion is strained off, leaving a stiff clay-like paste that can be wrapped in waxed paper or cloth, put into tin boxes, and kept in a cool, dry place. It will then keep its fermenting qualities for some time, but it must not be allowed to become dry, or it will be useless. By adding a little water to a portion of the paste it will, if kept properly, be always ready for use.

In the old days, when one could not buy yeast, it was the practice to twist up sticks of hazel wood so that they were full of apertures, and to steep them in the yeast during fermentation. They were then dried and used in the wort of the next brewing instead of yeast. However, one has to have yeast to work with, and it is possible to make it by adding two ounces of brown sugar to one pound of well-mashed mealy potatoes and two spoonfuls of common yeast, mixing them with warm water, and keeping the paste warm while fermenting. This will yield a quart of good yeast.

Another way to manufacture yeast is to boil a pound of flour, a quarter of a pound of raw sugar, and a small tablespoonful of salt, in two gallons of water for an hour. When it is milkwarm bottle it and cork it tight. It can be used in twenty-four hours, but you will need four times as much of it as of brewer's yeast.

Fermentation

You are now ready to proceed with the most important part of brewing—fermentation. The wort should have reached 72° to 75° before it is run from the coolers into the tun tub. Dissolve two-thirds of the brewer's yeast in a portion of the wort at a temperature of 85°, and when it has commenced to ferment, add another and equal portion to it. A vigorous fermentation will shortly commence, when the dissolved yeast should be poured over the whole of the fermenting tun before the wort is run in and incorporated with it. The remaining third of the yeast is fed to the tun as the occasion requires, to stimulate fermentation when it becomes languid, and to prevent the evil of over-yeasting the worts. The habit of putting all the yeast in the tun tub at once is a bad one and should be avoided. Fermentation should not go ahead too hastily.

The morning after the wort has been run into the tun tub it should have a slight cream on the surface. Fermentation should be very gradual at first or it will exhaust itself before the wort has been reduced to the desired state. Mix the white cream with the wort and take a portion from the tun for a saccharometer and thermometer test. Examine the tun again in the evening, and if fermentation is inactive add a small portion of yeast. Next morning, if fermentation is vigorous, you will find a cauliflower head with patches of dark brown yeast on it. Remove the patches of yeast, for if they were to remain they would impart a bitter, disagreeable taste to the beer. The white part of the head is again mixed with the mass, and another sample is tested with the saccharometer and thermometer. After this the head is not disturbed, but further samples of the wort are taken out from time to time for testing.

When a dark brown head, having a uniform appearance, and inclined to fall rather than to rise, replaces the white one, it is skimmed off and the beer is casked or "fined." If this head should fall to the bottom before it is skimmed it would give the beer a flavor called "yeast-bitten" and would prevent its fining in the casks. If there is the slightest sign of the brown head falling it ought to be skimmed at once. No part of brewing is so critical, or needs more attention than this.

After skimming take another portion of the wort for examination. If attenuation has not reached the desired point, which should be one-half, or at least two-fifths of its original gravity, it should be stimulated and skimmed every two hours until this is attained.

When the beer is casked fermentation must be invigorated again. Mix one-half pound of flour with a quarter of a pound of salt and heat them, but do not let them brown. Add this mixture to the wort in the fermenting tun just before it is drawn off.

Beer Casks

The casks must be perfectly clean and dry. Place them on the stands, a little off the perpendicular. The greatest attention must be paid to filling the casks, that the yeast may be able to discharge itself from the beer by way of the bung-hole. Were the filling-up neglected, the yeast, instead of discharging itself, would fall to the bottom, rendering the beer harsh and unpleasant, and causing new fermentation at every change of the weather. This is the reason why so much home-brewed beer is thick and muddy. Meticulous care at this point will also avoid the necessity of fining with isinglass, which always tends to impoverish and flatten the beer.

Do not touch the casks during fermentation, but when it has ceased they should be moved to the cellar, and so placed upon stands as to allow the beer to be easily drawn from them. If you make your beer in March, and intend to keep it over the summer, you should take old ale, mixed with the finest hops procurable, and place some in each cask in the proportion of four ounces of hops to each eighteen gallon cask. When the casks are moved from the brewhouse to the cellar, the beer will be agitated and new fermentation will take place, and this should be allowed to subside before the hops are added. After the hops are put in the casks are closed with wooden bungs that are driven in tightly. A spile hole should be made in each cask and a vent plug inserted loosely. In a day or two the vent plug can be firmly driven in.

Table Beer

The table beer run into the copper from the second extraction, and boiled with the strained boiled hops for an hour and a half, is now drawn off through a sieve into the cooler. When the temperature of the wort reaches 75° a portion is taken out and tested with the saccharometer. A gallon of wort from the cooler at a temperature of 85° is mixed with a quart of brewer's yeast. At the end of half an hour, when fermentation will have begun, this mixture is poured into the fermenting tun, and the wort is let down on it at a temperature of 75°. The next morning it is casked, and filled up as often as the first lot to be made. Fermentation will stop in about forty-eight hours, when the casks can be bunged and moved to the cellar.

Fining

If the beer is cloudy and thick when casked it will have to be fined. Fining should not be used unless it is absolutely necessary, as it always makes beer flat and increases acidity, especially if the cellar is warm or the beer is weak. When it is essential to fine your beer it may be done by dissolving one ounce of isinglass in a quart of stale beer and allowing it to stand for several days, when a second quart may be added, the whole strained through a sieve, and a half pint of the mixture stirred into each eighteen-gallon barrel of beer. Bung the casks tightly, and the beer will be fit to drink in a few days.

In order to know if beer is in the proper condition to be fined, draw off some into a pint bottle or a large glass and add a teaspoonful of finings. Shake the mixture and then let it stand. If the beer is ready to fine, you will see that in a few minutes the isinglass collects the feculencies of the beer into large fleecy masses that settle to the bottom of the container. If the beer is not ready fermentation will still be going on and the bulk of the finings will sink to the bottom, leaving the beer still foul, except just at the top, where there will be a little transparency.

Egg shells put into beer will not only fine it, but are also said to prevent it from becoming acid. The best way to avert acidity is to exclude air from the beer while it is in the cask, and to keep it in a dry, cool cellar. Protect the bung hole with an iron pad, over which you should work a piece of clay big enough to cover it. THE PUBLICAN'S OWN BOOK, AND DOMESTIC BREWER'S GUIDE says to suspend a knob of marble by a tape from the bung hole to near the bottom of the cask. "The marble being nothing more than pure carbonate of lime, the acidity of the beer acts upon the marble, and thus becomes neutralized and prevents the beer from turning sour. In some experiments the marble has been found considerably eaten away, except where it was surrounded by the tape, and the beer remain sound until the last."

Old Brewing Secrets

To restore a barrel of sour or stale beer, put in one quarter of a pound of hops, and two pounds of chalk in the bung-hole. In a few days it will draw off perfectly fresh. Another way is to mix a small teaspoonful of soda with every quart you drink just before you drink it. Some persons hang a linen bag full of pounded oyster shells inside the barrel.

Two or three sea biscuits, or pilot biscuits, put in a bag with some hops, and suspended in the barrel, will give beer a good flavor.

To give new ale the flavor of old, take the bung from the barrel and insert there a sliced Seville orange.

To cure beer or prevent foxing, cut a handful of hyssop into small pieces, mix it with a handful of salt, and put this into the barrel. Stir the beer up well and stop the barrel tightly. Or, you can infuse a handful of hops with water and a small amount of salt of tartar in boiling water. When it is cold, strain off the liquor, pour it all into the cask, and drive in the bung.

It is important to know how to sweeten tainted casks, and season new ones. When casks have become tainted or foxed it is difficult to restore them to usuable condition. Such casks should be saved for inferior ale or table beer. Unhead the bad cask and put in a chafing dish of hot coals, on which you will throw pitch or brimstone. While the cask is being fumigated the head should be put on loosely. You can also clean the inside of the cask with a scrubbing brush and a strong ley made from wood ashes. Pour in the ley through the bung-hole, boiling hot, and let it remain for some time. Malt dust boiled in water, or bay salt, is sometimes used.

The old method of cleaning a musty cask was to fill it nearly to the brim with boiling water, and then put in some pieces of unslacked stone lime. The lime will immediately effervesce, but this action must not be allowed to continue for more than a half an hour, or the lime will give the cask as bad a taste as would the must. When the effervescence is over, bung down, but wash out the cask before the liquor is quite cold.

If casks are only slightly tainted, put in some powdered charcoal, fill them almost full with boiling water, drive in the bung, roll them around, and then let them stand until they are cold. Wash out the casks, and the charcoal will be found to have absorbed the taint and left the casks pure.

The wood of new casks will impart its flavor to the beer for several brewings unless measures are taken to prevent it. First wash the casks in cold, and then in boiling water. Afterwards scald them with salt and water boiled together. Or, after they are well washed, keep beer-grounds or stale beer in them. Coopers season the staves by boiling them in a copper before they are made into casks. Barrels must be kept close bunged when they are empty or they will get foul.

I trust that the outline of old-time brewing that I have given you will quicken your interest in the art. It has been a difficult task to compress a description of how our forefathers brewed into such a short talk. You will doubtless want to delve deeper into the science. There are weighty tomes to be found in which you can carry out research on any phase of brewing practise. All that I have attempted to do is to give you a working knowledge of what went on when an old-time beer was made. You will want to add constantly to your store of information, and the proverb that "art is long, but life is short" applies to brewing as well as to painting, sculpture or literature. Study and experimentation should be your constant aim, that you may continually improve your methods and your brews. May you remain steadfast in your brewing, so that you can say to our brethren of solemn mein who would regulate our drinking:

> *"Dost thou think, because thou art virtuous, there shall be nor more cakes and ale?"*

❧ RECIPES & CURIOUS LORE OF THE OLDEN TIME BREWING.

An Address before the Special Meeting, December 19, 1931. By The Rev. Enoch Bailey Rhodes, D.D.

Felix qui potuit rerum cognoscere causas.

FELLOWS OF THE SOCIETY: Let me congratulate you on your intrepidity in braving the winds and snows of a Vermont blizzard in order that you might have the privilege of listening to the words of wisdom I am about to utter. I am flattered, gentlemen, but at the same time I am vain enough to feel that the old-time recipes I have gathered so lovingly will repay you for having floundered through drifts and skidded down icy hills. I am inclined to think that no other devotion but that to good beer and all it implies could induce so many of you to leave the warm comforts of your firesides on such a night. Your enthusiasm does you honor!

When you return to your homes, if you are able to get there, I trust you will find numerous cheering bottles, products of a perfect brew, to warm the cockles of your hearts—not to mention nipped noses and frosted toes—before you snuggle between the sheets to dream of the quaint lore that you are now to hear.

As the old song says:

> *He that drinketh strong beer*
> *And goes to bed right mellow,*
> *Lives as he ought to live*
> *And dies a hearty fellow.*

Essences & Spices

And now for the business of the evening! First of all, I want to explain that certain essences and spices will be mentioned during my discourse. It might be well to go over some of these first.

ALLSPICE or PIMENTO is the immature fruit of the *Eugenia pimenta* which combines the flavor of nutmegs, cloves, and cinnamon. To make it into an essence, pound some allspice, put it into a two-ounce bottle, fill the bottle with spirits of wine, digest, and strain.

ANISEED ESSENCE is made by infusing bruised seeds of anis in spirit, or by mixing one ounce of aniseed oil with two ounces of rectified spirits.

ESSENCE OF CITRON consists of thirty drops of oil of citron with one ounce of proof spirit.

ESSENCE OF SPRUCE is prepared from the young tops of the *Pinus larix,* boiled until it evaporates to a thick syrup. This, fermented with molasses, makes spruce beer. It can also be made by boiling the young tops of black spruce-fir (*Abies nigra*) and concentrating by evaporation.

CASPSICUM was used because "it disperses wind and crudities caused by indigestion. It also gives a warm glow to the stomach, but should be carefully employed." An excellent dyspeptic for a night like this! It should be almost as warming as the concoction of a reverend gentleman of Virginia, who added some sugar and a teaspoonful of curry powder to a pint of milk and drank it boiling hot!

ESSENTIA BINAE is sugar boiled in an iron vessel till it becomes a thick, black, and extremely bitter syrup.

COLOR is composed of moist sugar boiled until it obtains a middle state between bitter and sweet. It is used to give porter the fine flavor and color which many admire.

The Recipes

Now I can go ahead with the recipes. The oldest drink with which we are conversant is metheglin (from the Welsh *Meddyglin*), or meathe. It was said that:

> *Our drowsy metheglin*
> *Was ordained only to inveigle in*
> *The nonce who knows not to drink it.*
> *But is fuddled before he can think it.*

Sir Kenelm Digby (or Digbie), doted on by that most convivial of kinsprits, Christopher Morley, says in his THE CLOSET OPENED:

To Make Excellent Meathe

To every quart of Honey, take two quarts of water. Put your water in a clean Kettle over the fire, and with a stick take the just measure, how high the water cometh, making a notch, where the superficies toucheth the stick. As soon as the water is warm, put in your Honey, and let it boil, skimming it always, till it be very clean; Then put to every Gallon of water, one pound of the best Blew-raisins of the Sun, first clean picked from the stalks, and clean washed. Let them remain in the boiling Liquor, till they be throughly swollen and soft; Then take them out, and put into a Hair-bag, and strain all the juice and pulp and substance from them in an Apothecaries Press; which put back into your liquor, and let it boil, till it be consumed just to the notch you took at first, for the measure of your water alone. Then let your liquor run through a Hair-strainer into an empty Wooden-vat, which must stand endwise, with the head of the upper-end out; and there let it remain till the next day, that the liquor be quite cold. Then Tun it into a good Barrel, not filled quite full, and let the bung remain open for six weeks. Then stop it up close, and drink not of it till after nine months.

This Meathe is singularly good for a Consumption, Stone, Gravel, Weak-sight, and many more things. A Chief Burgo-master of Antwerpe, used for many years to drink no other drink but this; at Meals and all times, even for pledging of healths. And though He were an old man he was of an ex-traordinary vigor every way, and had every year a Child, had always a great appetite and good digestion; and yet was not fat.

This recipe is taken *verbatim* from the edition of 1669. The last part should be as good a recommendation as one could want for any-thing.

Another old recipe for metheglin calls for ingredients most of us can never hope to get, but it is quaint enough to warrant my giving it to you.

Metheglin

Take all sorts of Hearbs that are good and wholesome as Balme, Mint, Fennel, Rosemary, Angelica, wilde Thyme, Isop, Burnet, Egrimony, and such other as you think fit; some Field Hearbs, but you must not put in too many, but especially Rosemary or any Strong Hearbs lesse than halfe a handful will serve of every sorte, you must boyl your Hearbs & strain them, and let the liquor stand till to Morrow and settle them, take off the clearest Liquor, two Gallons & a halfe to one Gallon of Honey, and that proportion as much as you will make, and let it boyle an houre, and in the boyling skim it very clear, then set it a cooling as you doe Beere, when it is cold take some very good Ale Barme and put into the bottome of the Tubb a thicke Setling that lyeth in the bottome of the Vessel that it is cooled in, and when it is all put together cover it with a Cloth and let it worke very neere three dayes, and when you mean to put it up, skim off all the Barme clean, put it up in to the Vessel, but you must not stop your Vessel very close in three or four dayes but let it have all the vent, for it will worke and when it is close stopped you must looke very often to it and have a peg in the top to give it vent, when you heare it make a noise as it will do, or else it will breake the Vessell; sometimes I make a bag and put in good store of Ginger sliced, some Cloves and Cinnamon and boyl it in, and other time I put it into the Barrel and never boyl it, it is both good, but Nutmeg & Mace do not well to my Tast.

Modern Metheglin

To some new honey (that which runs from the comb is best) add spring water; put in an egg; boil this liquor till the egg swims above the liquor, strain; clear, and pour in a cask. To every 15 gallons add 2 ounces of bruised ginger, 1 ounce cloves and mace, one and one-half ounces cinnamon, all bruised together and tied up in a muslin bag; accelerate the fermentation with yeast; when worked sufficiently bung up; in six weeks draw off into bottles.

Sir Kenelm Digby also instructs us how:

To Make Ale Drink Quick

When smalle Ale hath wrought sufficiently, draw into bottles; but first put into every bottle twelve good raisins of the Sun split and stoned. Then stop up the bottle close and set it in sand or a cold dry Cellar. After a while this will drink exceedingly quick and pleasent. Likewise take six Wheat-corns, and bruise them, and put into a bottle of Ale; it will make it exceeding quick and stronger.

The sixth edition of THE COUNTY HOUSEWIFE, by R. Bradley, London, 1762, gives the following recipe for Mead:

To Make Mead, From Lady G.

Take eight Gallons of Water, and as much Honey as will make it bear an Egg; add to this the Rinds of six Lemmons, and boil it well, scumming it carefully as it rises. When 'tis off the Fire, put to it the Juice of the six Lemmons, and pour it into a clean Tub, or earthern Vessel, if you have one large enough, to work three days; then scum it well, and pour off the clear into the Cask, and let it stand open till it has done making a hissing Noise; after which stop it up close, and in three months time it will be fine, and fit for bottling.

I had better explain that "to bear an egg" means to float an egg.

Another way to make mead was to boil the combs from which the honey had been drained with sufficient water to make a tolerably sweet liquor. Ferment the liquor with yeast after pouring it into a cask, and when it has worked enough bung up the cask. In six weeks it can be drawn off and bottled. Sack mead is made by adding brandy and hops to the comb liquor.

The true difference between metheglin and mead is that the former is made from honey while the latter is made from honeycombs. The terms are sometimes used interchangeably, and the name mead has even been given to drinks such as that I am about to tell you how to make, but which is in no sense real mead.

Mead

WATER	3 *pints*
SUGAR	1½ *pints*
MOLASSES	½ *pint*
CREAM OF TARTAR	2 *ounces*
ESSENCE OF SASSAFRAS	1 *ounce*

Pour the water, boiling, on the sugar and molasses, and let this stand until it is almost cold. Now add the tartar and the sassafras. When it is quite cold it is ready to bottle. When this mead is drunk, put a tablespoonful in a glass. Fill the glass two-thirds full with cold water. Now stir in a little soda. The mead should be drunk while it is foaming. Mead is a summer drink, like ginger-beer.

Sandow's Mead

Be sure to get soft water. Heat about 10 gallons of it to milk warm temperature, then start to dissolve honey into it, until enough honey is there so that the mixture will bear an egg, then boil easily for an hour, skimming off the scum from time to time. Now you should add half a spoonful of mace, 2 of nutmeg, 4 sticks of cinnamon, 2 of ginger, one quarter of an ounce of pepper, and put them together into the honey-water mixture. Then add 1 lemon and a sprig of sweetbriar and rosemary. Do not leave the sprigs of rosemary and sweetbriar in very long. Let the mixture stand about twenty hours, then strain off into a barrel, put the spices left in a bag, and hang the bag from the top of the barrel, but not in the liquid; then bung up the barrel for three months. Then you can bottle it.

You must wonder why I have bored you with all this talk of metheglin and mead. I realize that what you want to hear about is how to make beer and ale that differs from the brews you have enjoyed making from the malt syrups that are so conveniently kept in stock at the corner grocery store. Be patient, I will relieve your anxiety in a moment. The ancient drinks of the Britons, Picts and Gauls are not to be laughed at. Try them. You will be pleasantly surprised.

Now for the beers. You have the rest of a long, cold winter in which to make them. They should just be in prime condition to assuage your thirst when you are despairing of being able to last out the scorching days of next summer. We will start with:

Poor Man's Beer

SOFT WATER	4½ *gallons*
MOLASSES	1 *quart*
YEAST	1 *cake*

Boil 2¼ gallons of soft water. Place 2¼ gallons of cold soft water in a barrel. Pour the boiling water into the barrel and then add to the warm water resulting 1 quart of good molasses and a crumbled up yeast cake. Let the bung hole of the barrel stay open until all fermentation ceases. Then bottle the beer or bung up the barrel.

Virginia Beer

WATER	9 *quarts*
HOPS	6 *ounces*
GINGER (POWDERED)	12 *spoonfuls*
MOLASSES	2 *quarts*
BREAD, DRY	½ *pound*
YEAST	2 *cakes*

Take the hops and put them in a copper pot with 5 quarts of water and boil for three hours. Then strain off the liquor into another vessel. Add 4 quarts of cold water and 12 spoonfuls of powdered ginger to the hops in the copper pot and let them boil for three hours, after which strain and add it to the first boiled liquor. Into this mixture, which will be about 9 quarts, add and stir well 2 quarts of good molasses. Now take a loaf of whole wheat bread, cut it up into slices, and toast them until they are hard, like Holland rusk. Crush the toast and add it to the liquor. After the mixture is cool add 2 yeast cakes. Put the liquor into a crock and let it stand until it has finished fermentation, which is shown by all froth having settled and the cessation of activity. The beer can now be bottled.

The Father of our Country loved his beer and wine as dearly as does any member of this honorable *Company*. About ten years ago a recipe for small beer was discovered in one of Washington's note books. It was probably written in 1757:

George Washington's Small Beer

Take a large sifter full of Bran Hops to your taste. Boil these 3 hours then strain out 30 Gall'ns into a Cooler, put in 3 Gall'ns Molasses while the Beer is Scalding hot or rather draw the Molasses into the Cooler & Strain the Beer on it while boiling hot. Let this stand till it is little more than

Blood warm then put in a quart of Yeast. If the Weather is very Cold cover it over with a Blanket & let it Work in the Cooler then put it into the Cask—leave the Bung open till it is almost done Working—Bottle it that day Week it was Brewed.

Elbulum or Elderberry Beer

Boil in 18 gallons of the finest and strongest wort 1½ pecks of elderberries which are quite ripe. Strain clear and when cold work the liquor in the barrel and let it remain there one year, at which time it may be bottled. You may add a few hops and some spices tied in a bag.

Hop Beer

HOPS	5 *ounces*
MOLASSES	1 *gallon*
WATER	2 or 3 *pails*

To make a barrel of beer, take 5 ounces of good hops, add two or three pails of water, simmer 6 hours, strain while hot into a barrel, add 1 gallon of molasses, and stir thoroughly. Fill the barrel with water and mix the whole together. The beer will be fit for use in about forty-eight hours. A less quantity may be made by the same rule, but always have the vessel in which you make it full, in order that the beer when it works may discharge the filth that rises to the surface.

THE NEW ENGLAND FARRIER, AND FAMILY PHYSICIAN, by Josiah Richardson, Exeter, Mass., 1828, contained the next four recipes.

Jumble Beer

GINGER, GROUND	2 *teaspoonfuls*
MOLASSES	1 *pint*
WATER	2½ *pails*

Mix the ginger and molasses with a little warm water, especially in cold weather; then add the whole compliment of water and shake it very briskly. In about six to eight hours it will be sufficiently fermented.

Hop Beer

Hops	1 *pound*
Molasses	½ *gallon*
Ginger, powdered	1 *teacupful*
Water	1½ *pailfuls*

For half a barrel of beer take a pound of hops and half a gallon of molasses; the latter must be poured by itself into the cask. Boil the hops five minutes, adding to them a teacupful of powdered ginger, in about a pailful and a half of water, that is, a quantity sufficient to extract the virtue of the hops. When sufficiently brewed, put it up warm into the cask, shaking it well in order to mix it with the molasses. Then fill it up with water quite to the bung, which must be left open to allow it to work. You must be careful to keep it constantly filled up with water when it works over.

Vermont Beer

Hops	4 *ounces*
Molasses	2 *quarts*
Emptings	1 *pint*
Water	

Take four ounces of hops and boil them in a sufficient quantity of water for three hours. Put the liquor in a clean barrel, and fill it with water after adding 2 quarts of molasses and a pint of emptings while the liquor is still warm. Let it stand twenty-four hours with the bung out a little, when it will be fit for use. Do it in this manner and it will be good and wholesome beer.

Brattleboro Beer

HOPS	1 *ounce*
GINGER, POUNDED	1 *ounce*
MOLASSES	4 *pounds*
YEAST	
WATER	

Boil the hops, ginger, and molasses in two gallons of water. When at the temperature of new milk, add yeast to ferment it in the manner of malt liquor. This is reported to be wholesome and agreeable, and is not only cheaper, but will keep much longer than common beer.

Treacle Beer

TREACLE (MOLASSES)	1½ *pounds*
HOPS	1 *ounce*
GINGER, BRUISED	¼ *ounce*
BAY LEAVES	3
YEAST	1 *ounce*
WATER	

In 8 quarts of boiling water put one and a half pounds of treacle, one quarter of an ounce of bruised ginger, 3 bay leaves, and 1 ounce of hops. Boil the infusion for an hour. Ferment with an ounce of yeast on a slice of bread. When fermenting is finished, bottle.

Now I will speak of some of the famous brews of old England and let you in on their manufacture.

Worcestershire Country Ale

MALT	2 *bushels*
HOPS	2 *pounds*
FRESH YEAST	1 *quart*

The malt, which should be ground rather coarsely, is to be douced in the mash tub, which has a drainage hole, with a spigot, at the bottom. The hole is covered with a sieve on the inside. The liquor (water) is boiled in the copper, and enough is then run in to cover the bottom of the mash tub to a depth of about two inches. Then half a bushel of malt is put in and stirred until it is completely saturated. Enough liquor is added to wet another half bushel of malt, which is now put in, and the whole is stirred so that every grain of malt is soaked. About a gallon of the liquor is now drawn off and thrown over the top of the malt in the mash tub, after which dry malt is sprinkled over it and it is let stand three hours for infusion.

Steep your hops in hot water in the underback, and when the mash has infused for three hours slowly draw off the wort from the mash tub to the underback. Add some more liquor (about the same quantity as before) to the mash until the whole is wet. This second infusion must stand in the tub one hour, when it is run off with the other liquor, put in the copper, and boiled for an hour. To make 24 gallons of ale you will need about 30 gallons of wort, which is made to that quantity by sprinkling hot water (sparging) on the malt in the mash tub while it is let drain slowly. The important thing is that the wort is cooled quickly and uniformly, which can be done by putting it in shallow vessels of the same size, filling them to an equal depth, and setting them in a cold place. If you have a brew house with regular coolers, so much the better. *Never mix hot wort with cold.*

Now stir a quart of fresh yeast with a gallon of milk-warm wort in the bottom of the fermenting tun. It will immediately begin to act, and as each portion of wort becomes sufficiently cool, add it to the fermenting tub, but reserve a few gallons for a later use. In this brew do not stir or remove the first or second head of yeast, but let it stay until the head is risen and has become very strong, when, before it begins to sink, it is cleaned off.

Before casking the ale, add to each barrel enough of the wort you have saved out to cover the bottom to a depth of one inch, the barrels being placed in an upright position. In a few days fermentation in the barrels will have ceased and they can be closely bunged. In another week put a handful of half-boiled hops in each barrel, which is then filled and bunged tight. Keep the ale about four months before tapping.

Shropshire Ale

MALT	5½ *bushels*
HOPS	6¼ *pounds*
YEAST	1 *quart*

First wash the barrels at midnight in cold water, scrubbing the insides well with a stiff brush or clean chain, so that they are clean and sweet. At the same time wash the tubs, coolers, and other utensils. After washing, the barrels and utensils must be scalded.

Weigh the hops, measure the malt, and fill the copper with water so you may begin your labors at two o'clock in the morning.

This recipe will give you 36 gallons of good ale. Mash 5½ bushels of malt, a bushel at a time, in the mash tub, using as much water at the usual temperature as will wet the malt. When all the malt has been put in, and has been well stirred with the mashing-oar, add 15 gallons of boiling water. Cover the mashing tub and let the mash infuse for three hours, then run the wort off into a cooler. Place 6¼ pounds of hops in the cooler. When all the liquor has been withdrawn from the mash tub pour 12 gallons more of boiling water on the malt, let it stand for an hour, then run that off also, until you have about 40 gallons of wort.

The fire under the copper must be extinguished before you pour in the wort, for a hot copper would discolor the ale. Put the wort in the cool copper, boil for one hour, and strain it through a hair sieve into the coolers. When it is cool, put a quart of ale yeast mixed with 6 gallons of wort in the fermenting tub and leave it to work until morning; then add more liquor and in the evening of that day put in the rest of the wort. The next morning cleanse it by skimming. Place a receptacle to catch what may work over, and when the ale has stopped working in the barrels, clear the ale which has worked out and fill the barrels with it. After the ale has been barreled and stood for eight or ten days rack it into another barrel, or the tun tub, that the barrel may be cleaned out with a dry cloth and the ale returned to it immediately. At this stage of the process add 3 quarts of hot hops from a previous brewing, but if you have not brewed recently it will be necessary to boil the quantity of hops you need and take them from their liquor. In this event the liquor can be used for table beer. When the hops have been put in, stop the barrel up closely, and cover the bung with wet sand.

Burton Ale

This famous brew is made from the palest of malt and hops, for if it is not as pale as straw it will not please the connoisseurs who dote on Burton brew. The chief cause for the distinctive excellence of Burton lies in the waters of the river Trent which run over rocks of gypsum. Since you cannot have the water of Trent which benificent Nature has especially prepared for this ale, you may make a more than passable imitation of it by using these materials:

SALT OF STEEL	2 *ounces* to 20 *barrels*
HONEY	1 *pound per barrel*
SULPHATE OF LIME	6 *ounces per barrel*
BLACK RESIN	1 *ounce per barrel*

The salt of steel (ferric salts) is dried until it becomes white and is then infused in twenty barrels of hot water before mashing. The quantity must be kept exact, as this is an extremely mischievous substance. The entire lot of liquor is then, at a temperature of between 165° and 170°, poured upon the malt. Mashing is continued about an hour, after which infusion is let take place an hour and a half longer, the tun being covered with a sack of dry malt to preserve the heat. When the first mash is run off, from 10 to 15 barrels of liquor, according to the proposed strength, is run over the malt at 185° and allowed to infuse for two hours, when it will have sunk and mixed with the malt without being mashed.

Now boil 6 pounds of hops in water for each quarter of malt. The hops should be boiled from two to two and a half hours. Ten to fifteen minutes before turning off, a pound of honey per barrel is put in the copper, the honey having previously been dissolved in scalding hot liquor.

To prepare for fermentation, a pound of solid yeast for each barrel must be added to the wort in the fermenting tun when it has cooled to 64° F. Skim off the first head to rid the wort of impurities floating on the surface. Now cover the tun, but stir up the wort two or three times a day. In forty-eight to sixty hours the wort should rise in temperature to 80° or more. When fermentation has proceeded to the point when the specific gravity is about 12 pounds, it is usual to put half a gallon of bean flour and 4 ounces of sal prunella, previously mixed with a portion of the wort, to every 20 barrels. The whole is now drawn off into barrels, which are filled up every two hours until they stop discharging any yeast. Should the fermenting tun fall in temperature during the process, some recommend that 2½ ounces of jalap be added for every 20 barrels of wort. At the moment the barrels have stopped working, mix 6 ounces of unburnt or bruised sulphate of lime with 1 ounce of black resin in some of the ale and put it into each barrel. Then a small quantity of half-boiled hops is to be inserted, and the barrel, being filled, is bunged up closely. A gimlet hole must be bored at the side of the bung and closed with a peg for the escape of carbonic gas as needed. The resin, hops and lime will prevent the access of atmospheric air and any secondary fermentation with consequent acidity.

The Burton brewers have asserted on oath that they use only water, malt, and hops in brewing their ale. The Trent river water contains the other necessary ingredients, and the rules for making this brew that I have given you are those which will allow you to make an ale similar to that of Burton which has been renowned for many centuries.

Scotch Ale

The brewing of Scotch ale is confined to the colder months of the year, owing to the low heat at which the tun is pitched for fermentation. This ale is pale, mild, free from bitterness, and the flavor of hops never predominates.

The Scotch take but one stiff mash for strong ale, making up the quantity by sparging. The sparges trickle successively through the goods and wash out as much more of the saccharine matter as may suffice for the intended strength of the ale, so that much more of the saccharine matter is extracted from the malt than would be possible by a second mashing.

The first step is to mash with the water at a temperature of 180° to 190°, varying with the dampness of the malt. Mash for twenty minutes to half an hour, then cover the tub and allow to infuse for three hours, after which the wort is to be drawn off into the copper in preference to draining into the underback. The first sparge is now made by spraying a barrel of water at 180° over the surface of the malt. The cock of the mash tub is opened to let off the wort into the underback in the manner of an ordinary mash.

When the first sparge is almost run off, another of equal amount is put on the malt, and successive sparges are conducted similarly until the wort in the underback, mixed with that in the copper, shows the desired gravity.

The quantity of hops seldom exceeds 4 pounds to the quarter of malt. A little honey as sweetening and a few coriander seeds for flavor are sometimes added.

The wort is boiled in the same way as for English ale, but a different process is followed after the wort is in the tun tub. The first heat of fermentation must be as low as possible, consistent with the action. The best heat is 50°, although some brewers start at 45° or 46° even in the coldest weather. The average length of time for fermentation is two weeks, although it sometimes takes as long as three. The quantity of yeast mentioned is generally enough, but in some cases an addition is made a day or two after if, in the judgment of the brewer, it seems desirable. The least amount of yeast that will carry forward fermentation is to be preferred, and to assure that purpose the tun is roused twice a day, morning and evening, to prevent its becoming too languid. With an increase in heat the weight of the wort diminishes, but finally the heat begins to lessen. When attenuation has become so slow as not to exceed half a pound in twenty-four hours, that is, when it has nearly ceased, the wort should be cleansed. If this were not done the formation of gas might be too weak to support the head, and the yeast, sinking to the bottom, would give the ale the disagreeable taste called "yeast-bitten."

To cleanse the ale, draw it off from near the bottom, that the head may continue to float on the surface until all the liquid has been casked. The Scotch, unlike the English, do not skim off the heads, but depend upon their presence to exclude the air. Ale thus cleansed throws off little or no yeast.

In a good fermentation there seldom remains more than a fourth of the original weight of the wort at the time of cleansing. If above a third is left the taste is generally mawkish. Scotch ale soon becomes fine, and is seldom racked.

Porter

To make six gallons of porter you will need:

MALT, GROUND	1 *peck*
HOPS	¼ *pound*
MOLASSES	¼ *pound*
LIQUORICE ROOT, GROUND	
SPANISH JUICE OR LIQUORICE	
ESSENTIA BINA	
CAPSICUM	
GINGER	
COLORING	

All the ingredients except the ginger are boiled with the first wort and produce that peculiar quality and flavor characteristic of porter. The ginger is added to the beer after it has worked. The heading is composed of equal parts of alum and ground copperas. Brew and ferment the porter the same as ale, and let it stand for three weeks, although it can be drunk after seven days. It needs to be worked quicker than ale, and the vent pegs must be kept loose in the barrels or they may burst. Porter must be fined, and one pint of finings is the usual allowance for thirty-six gallons, though sometimes more or less will be needed.

Ale from Sugar

A pure and pleasant ale can be made from sugar, without the use of malt. White sugar is best, but any kind will do. The cask to be used must have no bung hole, but must have a cock fixed in one of the staves far enough from the bottom to let the liquor run out but leave the sediment behind. In the center of the top bore a hole large enough to admit a bottle cork.

If you use a nine-gallon cask, and want a fairly strong ale, boil a trifle less than a pound and a half of hops in ten gallons of water for five minutes, or boil them in two or three gallons of water, making up the quantity required by the addition of more boiling water. Strain the liquor from the hops, dissolve in it thirteen pounds of sugar, add a pint of good yeast, and pour the whole into the cask, where it will soon begin to ferment. Fermentation will continue, in summer weather, for from three weeks to a month. During the last two weeks a cork should be lightly placed in the hole in the top of the cask, removing it every two or three days to let the gases escape. When fermentation is at an end the taste of sugar will be scarcely perceptible: the cork can then be driven in tightly and in four days the ale will be fit for drinking or bottling. A darker color can be given the ale by adding a little burnt molasses or sugar. This ale improves with age, especially when bottled.

As the hills of New England are covered with forests of pine and spruce, it is but natural that the people who live among them should be fond of spruce beer. There are two kinds of spruce beer, brown and white, but the latter is usually preferred. I will now describe several different ways of making spruce beer.

Spruce Beer, I

Dissolve 7 pounds of loaf sugar in 4½ gallons of hot water. When the heat has fallen to about 90° mix in 4 ounces of spruce gum and dissolve it by stirring. Then add one half pint of stiff brewer's yeast and mix thoroughly. Fermentation will soon commence in the summer, but in the winter you will need to excite it by keeping the cask in a warm room. When fermentation languishes the beer is ready to be drawn off, after which the cask is washed and the liquor is returned to it. A new fermentation begins, at the end of which the beer is bottled. To make brown spruce beer, use brown sugar or molasses instead of loaf sugar.

Spruce Beer, II

To 6 gallons of water add 2 quarts of molasses, 3 ounces of hops, 2 ounces of allspice, three-quarters of a pound of bruised ginger, and 6 ounces of essence of spruce. Boil the ginger, hops and allspice in the water for an hour, then strain into a cask while warm. Stir in one half a pint of good yeast, and when fermentation has ceased bung up the cask. In six days you can bottle the beer.

The next three recipes are from THE NEW-ENGLAND COOKERY, OR THE ART OF DRESSING ALL KINDS OF FLESH, FISH, AND VEGETABLES, AND THE BEST MODES OF MAKING PASTES, PUFFS, PIES, TARTS, PUDDINGS, CUSTARDS AND PRESERVES, AND ALL KINDS OF CAKES, FROM THE IMPERIAL PLUM TO PLAIN CAKE, PARTICULARLY ADAPTED TO THIS PART OF OUR COUNTRY. COMPILED BY LUCY EMERSON, MONTPELIER: PRINTED FOR JOSIAH PARKS, 1808. Surely they ought to be good when taken from a book with such a mouth-filling title!

Spruce Beer, III

To make spruce beer out of the essence, take seven ounces of essence of spruce and fourteen pounds of molasses for an eighteen gallon cask. Mix them with a few gallons of hot water and pour into the cask. Then fill the cask with cold water, stir well, make it about luke warm, and add two-thirds of a pint of good yeast or the grounds of porter. Let it stand for four or five days to work, then bung it up tight. Two or three days later it will be fit for bottling and immediate use.

Spruce Beer, IV

To make spruce beer out of shed spruce. To one quart of shed spruce add two gallons of cold water, and so on in proportion to the quantity you wish to make. Then add one pint of molasses to every two gallons, let it boil four or five hours and stand until it is luke warm. Then put one pint of yeast to ten gallons, let it work, and cask it. Bung the cask tight and in two days the beer will be fit for use.

Spruce Beer, V

Take four ounces of hops, let them boil half an hour in one gallon of water, and strain the hop water. Add sixteen gallons of warm water, two gallons of molasses, eight ounces of essence of spruce dissolved in a quart of water, and pour into a clean cask. Shake the mixture well together and add half a pint of emptings. Let it stand and work one week. If the weather is very warm less time will do. When you bottle this beer put one teaspoonful of molasses in each bottle.

THE NEW-ENGLAND COOKERY, *etc., etc.,* from which I have been quoting seems to have had an adventurous life. It reappears in 1814 with very slight changes in the title. Poor Lucy! Her father and mother must have joined the "dear departed" in the intervening six years, for the author is now stated to be "an American Orphan." The proprietor is no longer Josiah Parks, but has become one William Fessenden, and the place of publication, instead of being Montpelier, is our own Brattleborough. Otherwise the book is substantially the same.

A well-known hot weather concoction of constant popularity was Ginger Beer. It was made according to numerous formulae, and has ever been a drink particularly dear to the English.

Simple Ginger Beer

LUMP SUGAR	3 *pounds*
GINGER, BRUISED	2 *ounces*
CREAM OF TARTAR	1 *ounce*
LEMONS	2 *sliced*
YEAST	4 *ounces*

Pour 4 gallons of water upon the above ingredients, except the yeast which is to be added last. Bottle after the beer has worked four days.

Quick Ginger Beer

SUGAR, WHITE	1 *pound*
GINGER, CRUSHED	1 *ounce*
CREAM OF TARTAR	2 *ounces*
YEAST	1 *cake*

Pour 1 gallon of boiling water over the moistened sugar, cream of tartar, and the ginger. Stir well, cover tightly, and let cool. After it has stood for ten or twelve hours add the yeast cake, which has been stirred in a cup of the liquor and let stand in a warm spot for five minutes. Stir in the dissolved yeast cake and re-cover the pot for exactly eight hours, at the end of which time you can skim, strain, and bottle the beer. You can drink it within twenty-four hours.

English Ginger Beer

GINGER, PULVERIZED	1½ *ounces*
CREAM OF TARTAR	1 *ounce*
SUGAR	1 *pound*
YEAST	1 *cake*

Add the ginger, cream of tartar, and sugar to three fourths of a gallon of warm water and boil for a few minutes. When the mixture is cold add the yeast cake. Pour the brew into a crock and cover it well with thick cloths. On the following day, strain the beer through a cloth and bottle it. If you cork it according to the English custom, be sure the corks are tied down securely. I suggest the use of caps, for this as for other beers. The ginger beer will be fit to drink in about four days.

Nettle Beer

This old and curious recipe was much used in New England even into the twentieth century. It was much used on farms in haying time. Take 2 pounds of ordinary nettles (Urticaceae) and boil down in water to a concentrated essence. Now add boiling water to make 3 gallons. To this add 3 pounds granulated sugar, the juice and sliced rinds of 3 lemons, ½ ounce ground ginger and 1 tablespoonful of cream of tartar. Let stand until lukewarm then add 1 yeast cake dissolved in warm water and keep this mixture in a crock until fermentation causes a head or foam. Skim off head and bottle. Fermentation will take place within 24 hours if crock is set in warm room 65°-70°. This beer will be ready to drink in two or three days.

Shandy-Gaff

Shandy-gaff, beloved drink of the English boatmen, consists of equal quantities of ginger beer and bitter beer mixed together. You may remember that Christopher Morley named one of his delightful volumes of essays *Shandy-Gaff*.

Jamaica Ginger Beer

Take 4 ounces of best Jamaica ginger pounded small, pour over it 5 gallons of boiling water, and allow it to stand until the heat has reached 80°; then strain it into a tub. Dissolve 6 pounds of refined sugar in the liquor with $1\frac{1}{2}$ ounces of cream of tartar and one half ounce of citric acid. If your brewing is being done in the summer, add one half pint of brewer's yeast at a heat of 80°, but if it is winter you will only need to keep your brew in a warm room to cause fermentation. When the beer has stopped fermenting, rack, then return to the cask to work for another day or two, when it may be drawn off, fined and bottled.

Cochin Ginger Beer

To $1\frac{1}{4}$ ounces cream of tartar add $1\frac{1}{2}$ ounces Cochin ginger which is bruised. Then 2 pounds loaf sugar, thin peel and juice of 2 lemons. Bruise the ginger and lemon peel with $\frac{1}{2}$ pound sugar in a mortar and put all together in a pan. To this add 6 quarts of boiling water and when lukewarm add 2 tablespoonfuls of good yeast. Let this ferment ten hours, drain clear and bottle. Can be drunk in ten hours.

African Ginger Beer

Bruise and macerate in 1 gallon of water, 6 ounces good African ginger with $\frac{1}{2}$ ounce capsicum pods. Boil this slowly for two hours and when almost cold add 9 pounds loaf sugar, 12 ounces cream tartar, 1 ounce essence of lemons and 1 ounce spirits of wine. Put all into the barrel and pour on 11 gallons boiling water. When this is lukewarm add the whites of 6 eggs whisked with a little of the liquor, and sufficient yeast to ferment. You may have to strain through tammy or flannel cloth or pass through filtering paper which has had some magnesia sprinkled on it. This transaction takes a long time but produces a fine article.

Dr. Pereira's Ginger Beer for Hot Climes

Take 5 pounds loaf sugar, ¼ pint lemon juice, ¼ pound honey, 5 ounces bruised ginger, 4 gallons water. Boil the ginger in 3 quarts of water for one hour; add the sugar, lemon juice and honey with the rest of the water; then strain clear. When cold add the whisked white of one egg and ½ teaspoonful of essence of lemon. Let stand four days and bottle.

Schultz's Ginger Beer

To 10 gallons of boiling water add 10 ounces cream of tartar, 15 ounces ground ginger, 10 lemons cut in slices. Boil, then let stand till nearly cool. Strain and press. Dissolve in this mixture 15 pounds sugar, and add when lukewarm 1 pint of yeast. Let all stand fourteen hours, skim, filter and bottle.

Imperial Pop

Take 3½ ounces cream of tartar, 4 ounces powdered ginger, 2 pounds sugar, 2½ ounces lemon juice, 2 gallons water. When lukewarm add 1 ounce German yeast, skim and bottle.

Ginger Beer with Raisins

To 1 pound raisins add ½ pound sugar, 1 ounce bruised ginger, ¾ ounce citric acid in powder form. Macerate the raisins and ginger in 2 quarts of water for one day, then boil for one hour. Add sugar, strain with pressure, adding the citric acid and bottle.

Twelve Months Ginger Beer

Take 3½ ounces bruised Jamaica ginger, 4 pounds loaf sugar, thin peel and juice of 2 lemons, 2 ounces powdered citric acid, 2 ounces German yeast, 2 gallons boiling water, and 10 drops essence of capsicum. Macerate the ginger in 1 quart of the water for one day. Add the sugar and 2 quarts of water, boil together and strain while warm. Boil the residue in 1 quart of water, strain and add to the liquor and rest of the water, which pour boiling hot on the lemon and citric acid. When lukewarm add capsicum and yeast on a crust of bread. Let it ferment two or three days, strain clear, add ¼ pint alcohol, and bottle in a fortnight.

Vermont Ginger Beer

LOAF SUGAR	2½ *pounds*
BRUISED GINGER	1½ *ounces*
CREAM OF TARTAR	1 *ounce*
THE RIND AND JUICE OF TWO LEMONS	
WATER	3 *gallons*
YEAST CAKES	2

The lemons should first be peeled, after which squeeze out and strain the juice of the lemons. Then put the ginger, the sugar, the cream of tartar and the rind and juice of the lemons into an earthen crock. On these various ingredients pour the boiling water. When this is almost cool, add the 2 yeast cakes. This should now be thoroughly stirred, and then placed, covered, in a warm place, as beside a stove. The following day skim off the surface of the liquid, and siphon into bottles, taking care not to disturb the yeasty sediment. The beer will be ready for use in three days. Ginger beer should be made only during the summer months.

Beer Wine

Beer is the wine of barley, and it is common knowledge to brewers and vintners that beer yeast and wine yeast are of an identical nature. So, despite the fact that we are brewers and not vintners, I will include a simple recipe for a homemade wine that utilizes the waste products of brewing.

When all the beer has been removed from the crock a yeasty sediment will remain. Scrape this out and put it into a two-gallon crock. Add one gallon of cold water, one pound of seeded raisins and three pounds of sugar. Stir this thoroughly and let it work for two weeks and then siphon, with a sponge-strainer siphon, into a gallon jug which should be loosely corked. After standing two or three days, there will be a slight sediment in the bottom of the jug; siphon it again into another jug, being careful not to disturb the sediment. Add three thimbles of sugar to the second jug.

The above will be a raisin wine, but many pleasant melodies can be played upon this simple theme. A quart of grape juice added along with the raisins gives a very happy result. Adding a dozen or two peaches with the raisins produces a magnificent peach wine. If it is not the peach season, add a jar of preserved peaches or a can of store peaches. The result will surprise you. Any of the other small fruits that are used for wine making, like elderberries, raspberries or cherries, may be used. In any case the raisins are always included. Like all wines, those described above will improve with age.

I realize that to make a palatable wine out of the waste products of beer making sounds very much like plucking a rabbit from a tall silk hat. But try it, as I did, and you will find it—not bad!

Old Malt-Drinks

When your cellar is stocked with the ales and beers you have brewed so lovingly and carefully, you should serve them in as many delectable ways as you can. Of course, good malt liquor is sufficient unto itself, and there are those who think it a desecration to tamper with it. Every man has his own opinion on the subject, and far be it from me to say you should or should not do this or that, but if you fail to make some of the decoctions possible to mix with ale and beer you will miss a lot of enjoyment. There are times when a mug of beer, pure and unadulterated, will be the only thing to fit your mood: but there should be other occasions when a little variety to your drinks will prove a pleasing change. The recipes I am about to give you are old, proven, and delicious. Try them.

"AULD MAN'S MILK," or HOT EGGNOG. Heat a pint of Scotch (or light) ale; add, while warming, ¼ ounce of bruised cinnamon, ¼ ounce grated nutmeg, ¼ ounce powdered ginger; beat up the yolks of 2 eggs with a little brown sugar; pour in the ale gradually; when well amalgamated, add a whiskey glass of whiskey.

ALEBERRY. Mix 3 spoonfuls of fine oatmeal with a quart of old ale; boil, strain clear, and sweeten; add juice of one lemon, ¼ grated nutmeg, some powdered ginger, and ½ pint of grape wine. Put a toast of bread on the surface of the liquor.

ALE POSSET. To a quart of ale add a round of buttered toast; let it soak in the ale; grate nutmeg on the bread, also sugar; add 1 pint of sherry, and serve hot.

" 'ARF-AND-'ARF." The London mixture is ½ pint of porter and ½ pint of ale; the New York, ½ pint of old ale and ½ pint of new.

ALE POSSET, "SIR WALTER RALEIGH'S." Take ½ pint of dry sherry (or white wine), ½ pint of good clear ale, add a quart of boiled cream, and strain through a tammy. This was a favorite remedy for colds, being a hot "nightcap."

EGG FLIP. Into a clean saucepan put 1 quart of good ale; then beat up in a bowl the yolks of 6 fresh eggs, into which grate half a nutmeg, and add ½ pound of moist sugar and a wineglass of gin or whiskey. Beat the eggs, nutmeg, sugar and liquor thoroughly. As the ale simmers, skim the froth off into the bowl containing the mixture. When the ale nearly boils (do not let it boil) pour it into the mixture, stirring the while. If you use the whites of eggs as well, only use 3 eggs.

LAMB'S WOOL. Roast 8 apples; mash them, and add 1 quart of old ale; press and strain; add ginger and nutmeg (grated); sweeten to taste, heat, and drink while warm.

WASSAIL BOWL. To 1 quart of hot ale add ¼ ounce each of grated nutmeg, ginger, and cinnamon; also ½ bottle of sherry, 2 slices of toasted bread, the juice and peel of 1 lemon, and two well roasted apples. Sweeten to taste.

HOT SPICED ALE. Boil 1 quart of good ale; add ½ grated nutmeg; beat up 2 eggs; mix them with a little cold ale; when ready, add the warm ale; keep stirring to a froth; add a piece of butter; serve with dry toast.

Ale and Beer Cups should be made with good sound ale, and drunk from tankards instead of glasses.

CAMBRIDGE ALE CUP. Boil in 3 pints of water 1 ounce of cloves, 1 ounce of cinnamon, 1 ounce of mace (all bruised together), for one hour. Then strain clear and add 3 ounces of powdered sugar, the juice and thin peel of a lemon, 3 pints of good college ale, and ½ pint of sherry. Heat immediately before serving and add a thin slice of fresh toast with some nutmeg grated on it.

ALE CUP. Macerate ¼ ounce of cinnamon, 2 cloves, 1 allspice, and a little grated nutmeg in a gill of sherry; in two hours strain, press, and put in a jug. Pour in 2 pints of Burton ale and 4 bottles of ginger beer. This is a drink that will make you forget all care. The addition of a little ice is an improvement.

JEHU'S NECTAR. Into a quart pot grate some ginger; add a wineglass of gin-and-bitters, then a pint of good ale, heated. This should be drunk while it is frothing.

ALE CUP. Bottle of ale, 2 bottles of ginger beer, ½ gill of syrup from preserved ginger, a slice of cucumber, and a pint of shaven ice. Mix together, stir well, and pour into thin glasses.

ALE CUP. A pint of good ale served with cracked ice.

PORTER CUP. A bottle of porter, wineglass of sherry, ½ bottle of claret, ½ nutmeg (grated), and sugar to taste. Mix the nutmeg and sherry, then strain in a quarter of an hour. Put the ingredients together in a jug with a slice of cucumber and a large lump of ice.

PORTER CUP. A bottle of Burton ale, a bottle of London porter, a pint of shaved ice, and a bottle of lemonade.

HOT CUP. Warm a pint of good ale; add 1 ounce of sugar, 1 ounce of mixed spices, and a glass of sherry. When nearly boiling, pour it in a round of buttered toast.

'TWEEN-DECKS CUP, or A SPLITTING HEADACHE. Put into ¼ pint of rum ½ dozen crushed cloves, a little cinnamon, ginger, and nutmeg; strain in an hour, with pressure; add equal quantities of lime juice and 2 quarts of bottled ale.

ALE CUP. Bottle of Scotch ale, mixed spice and nutmeg on a piece of toasted bread; pour through a strainer, on a lump of ice, and drink.

ALE CUP. Grate ¼ ounce of nutmeg; then add an equal quantity of pounded ginger, cinnamon, and 3 ounces of brown sugar; beat these up with the yolks of 3 eggs. Meanwhile warm ½ gallon of ale and ½ pint of gin. Pour the ingredients in together and whisk the spice mixture while the ale and gin are being added. When the cup is frothing it must be drunk immediately.

WAIT A BIT. Pint bottle of the best Scotch ale, 1 bottle of aerated lemonade, and a pint of cracked ice.

MOTHER-IN-LAW. Half old and half bitter ale.

COOPER. A pint of stout and a pint of porter.

EARLY BIRDS, or PURL. Heat a quart of ale mixed with a table-spoonful of powdered ginger and nutmeg; whisk up with a gill of cold ale, 2 ounces of moist sugar, and 3 eggs. When well frothed up add the warm ale, by degrees, and a glass of spirits. When this is done, drink without delay.

PLANTER'S MUG. Put into a covered jug the juice of two lemons, the finely cut peel of one lemon, one large glass of sherry, one glass of syrup (made by boiling one pound of loaf sugar with one and a half pints of water one-quarter of an hour), one pint of water, a handful of mint, and grated nutmeg. Ice for fifteen minutes, remove the mint, and add a bottle of ale.

COLONEL BYRD'S NIGHTCAP. Add ½ pint of strong ale and a wineglass of brandy to four lumps of sugar on which have been dropped four drops of essence of cloves. Serve hot and drink when going to bed.

ALE POSSETT. Mix a quart of cream with a pint of ale, then beat the yolks of ten eggs and the whites of four. Add the beaten eggs to the cream and ale, sweeten to taste, and flavor with nutmeg. Heat the mixture, stirring it constantly. When it becomes thick, but before it boils, remove it from the fire and serve.

I could go on giving you recipes "far, far into the night," but they would be no better than those I have seen you scribbling down so industriously as I read them to you. Later, perhaps, we will have a report on what you have done with them, and a comparative test—a practical test by way of foaming tankards—of your individual efforts. Then I expect to drink deep and let someone else do the talking. By the way, I wonder if you all realize how great a thirst prolonged use of the voice can raise? I assure you it is nothing to laugh at. I can't continue another minute. Besides, who knows how deep the drifts are now? If we tarry much longer I hate to think of the possible consequences. I can see a large collection of bottles and copious glasses on the table in the other room. Brothers, let us adjourn!

❧ A BIBULOUS GLOSSARY OF OLD & NEW WORDS & TERMS, WITH NOTES ON THEIR MANY NEW USAGES. Compiled by Dr. Behrens, and read by him at a private meeting of the officers of the Company on December 30, 1931.

NOTE. After the Master and the two Wardens of *The Company* had spent one long day over the completed manuscripts of the proceedings of this society, the Senior Warden arose and read the following from notes he had jotted down during the day. They are, I believe, of common interest to all members and while not a part of the proceedings of the society, it was thought best, in view of their lively interest, to include them here.

THE SECRETARY

ARVA. Beer brewed from the roots of pepper, made in all the islands of the South Pacific.

APPLE-JACK. A distilled liquor made from cider. Farmers do not bother in some regions to distill it, but instead let a barrel of hard cider freeze and then draw off the unfrozen center which will be almost pure alcohol. Apple-jack is the mainstay of serious drinkers in many rural districts and is also in great demand in and around New York City. Most of the "apple," as it is called, drunk in New York is a product of the farms of New Jersey where it is called "Jersey Lightning" for reasons that will be evident if you drink enough. In some sections the distilled product of cider is called cider brandy to distinguish it from the frozen-heart product called apple-jack. The names are used interchangeably, however, although many will continue to believe that cider brandy should only be applied to cider distilled twice. At any rate this liquid is a preferable substitute for good spirits and is a vast improvement over bad whiskey, gin, etc. Technically, cider brandy is the distilled product of cider wine. It is colorless or "white" when new, but turns a rich amber when stored in oak casks. The term apple-jack, used loosely today, was probably a colloquial expression but eventually came to be employed to designate any liquor distilled from cider.

ALCOHOLOMETER. A hydrometer for determining the strength of alcohol or the percentage of absolute alcohol in liquors.

ATTEMPERATOR. A device for regulating the temperature of wort during fermentation.

ATTENUATION. The conversion of the sugar of the malt into spirit, and the consequent reduction of the specific gravity of the fluid in the fermenting tub from this change.

AUDIT ALE. A kind of ale brewed, originally for audit day, in certain English colleges.

BACKS. a. Large vessels of any kind intended to hold wort. The term is probably a corruption of the French *basque,* which signifies the same thing. b. *Liquor back.* The water cistern to supply the brewery. c. *Underback.* Vessel to receive the wort when let off from the mash tub. d. *Hop back.* The first vessel for the wort to cool in, where the wort is drained from the hops. This is also sometimes called the *Jack back.*

BAR. An altar at which the weary, dispirited and a-thirst were wont to worship. It consisted of a long, flat expanse of mahogany supported by a base at the foot of which was a brass rail. The officiating priest stood behind the bar and poured forth libations for the supplicants on the other side. The ritual comprised putting one foot on the rail, lifting the oblation on high, and then drinking with impressive ceremony.

It is now faced by high stools on which *debutantes* and other females sit while having their afternoon "tea."

BAR-FLY. A bar-fly is no relation to the winged nuisance that commits suicide in your glass of beer when you let it stand too long in the summer. In all probability a bar-fly will never acquire wings either in this world or the next. It was thought this species would become extinct after 1920, but in the seclusion of any speakeasy they are still found in large numbers with one foot on a brass rail and continuous mixtures of what-have-you passing from hand to mouth.

BARTENDER. A gentleman of the old school, now largely resident in Paris, Havana, and other foreign cities. The bartender of aforetime was an encyclopedia of information and wit, a Chesterfield in manner, and a diplomat of the first rank. He was a chemical genius whose inventions brought more joy to living than have all the discoveries of laboratories. He was the friend of the friendless, the sympathetic confidant of secrets and sorrows. His modern namesake is but a poor imitation of one who was an honored ornament to society.

ye carnival up to date

BARROOM. A place of cheer formerly confined to masculine members of the *genus homo*. The old barrooms had a great influence on the artistic sensibilities of their habitues. Crystal chandeliers, enormous mirrors, faceted cut-glass, polished mahogany, and rows of varicolored bottles enchanted the eye. Lithographs of John L. Sullivan, Tom Sharkey, Jim Jeffries, Jack Johnson, Salvator and Nancy Hanks developed an appreciation of prints; while oil paintings of recumbent, undraped ladies added just the right high-brow touch. Nor was literature ignored, for the pink *Police Gazette* was always perused with avidity. Alas! the speakeasy bar is far, far different! They try to imitate the old-time atmosphere, but it is a hollow gesture. The female of the species has adopted it as her own, and man's last sanctuary is invaded.

BEER FLOAT. An instrument of the hydrometer type for ascertaining the percentage of alcohol in a mash.

BEER PUMP. A nearly obsolete instrument used for furnishing sufficient pressure to draught beers and ales so that they would flow freely when drawn off for serving. In New York they can still be hired by those who give beer parties.

BITTER ALE. A strong, bitter ale made from hops.

BITTERN or BITTERING. An intensely bitter mixture of quassia, cocculus Indicus, tobacco, etc., used by unscrupulous brewers in adulterating beer.

BLINK-BEER. Beer that has been kept unbroached until it is sharp.

BLINKED. A species of acetification to which beer is liable.

BOCK BEER. An especially strong German beer formerly popular in the United States. It is dark in color, not particularly bitter, and has a high alcoholic content. It is brewed in winter from the first of the new crops of hops and malt and is drunk in the spring. It was first made in Eimbeck, originally Eimbock, Prussia, a place famous for its breweries during the Reformation. In France bock is the name in general use for all beers.

BOOTLEGGER. A title of the new American aristocracy, bestowed for conspicuous service to the nation. When the Great Thirst came to us, and the country threatened to become as arid as Death Valley, the bootleggers rescued us from a dire fate. Bootleggers have a well-developed sense of public responsibility, and are confirmed prohibitionists. They support the dry members of Congress at all times, even in the lobbies and cloak rooms of the Senate Chamber. They supply the "best liquor you can get," "right off the boat," or "just come from Canada," and the fact that it was actually made in a noissome cellar is merely one of those trade secrets that everybody knows but chooses to ignore.

BOTTLED BEER. The following is a version of how the bottling of beer originated. "Dean Newall, of St. Paul's, in the reign of Queen Mary, was an excellent angler. But while Dean Newall was catching of fishes, Bishop Bonner was bent on catching of Newall, and would certainly have sent him to the shambles had not a good London merchant conveyed him away upon the seas. Newall was fishing on the banks of the Thames when he received the first intimation of his danger, which was so pressing he did not dare go back to his house to make preparations for his flight. Like an honest angler, he had taken provisions for the day; and when, in the first years of England's deliverance, he returned to his own country, and his old haunts, he remembered that, on the day of his flight, he had left a bottle of beer in a safe place on the bank of the stream in which he had fished; there he looked for it, and 'found no bottle, but a gun,' for such was the sound emitted at the opening thereof."

BRISKNESS of ale or beer is that state in which there is a quantity of carbonic acid compressed in it, which flies off when exposed to the air.

BUCKING. See *Foxing*.

BUNG-STARTER. An implement about which you do not hear as much as you used to. It was supposed to be an aid to the removal of bungs from beer kegs, but its principal utility seems to have been that of subduing fractious customers who refused to go home to the wife and kiddies without having an old-fashioned brawl before they left. A skilled bartender could wield a bung-starter with a combined efficiency and *sang-froid* that settled arguments when they were scarcely begun.

BUTTER ALE. An ale containing no hops or other bitter element, but flavored with sugar, butter and spices.

CERES. In classical mythology, the goddess of the grains, hence of brewing. The Romans called beer *cerevisia,* after Ceres, and the modern Spanish word for beer, *cervesa,* is derived from it.

CHICA. A South American beer made from fermented malt of Indian corn. Also a drink of high alcoholic content and amazing reactions obtainable by allowing sugar cane juice to ferment.

CIDER. The farmer's delight. When hard cider can be had for so little work and expense why should the farmer bother about prohibition? Not only that, he can get rich by making apple-jack to sell to poor souls from the city. Is it any wonder the inhabitants of rural districts vote dry, when it is so easy for them to drink wet and make money in the bargain?

COCKTAIL. Any one of hundreds of pernicious concoctions that have made America stomach-conscious. A fine disguise for the raw taste of synthetic liquor, and the steam that turns the wheels of nearly every party. The reason why young girls tell all, and speakeasy proprietors buy Rolls-Royces.

COPPER. a. *Liquor copper.* Copper for heating water. b. *Wort copper.* Copper for boiling the wort and hops.

CUCKOO ALE. An ale reserved for spring when the notes of the cuckoo are first heard.

ENTIRE. The original name for porter. Being drawn from one cask, it was called entire, or, entire butt. Malt liquors previously in use were ale, beer, and twopenny. It was then customary to call for a tankard of three thirds (or three threads), which was a mixture of a third each of beer, ale, and twopenny. In 1722 a brewer named Harewood made a liquor he called *entire,* meaning a combination of the three kinds mentioned above. It was first sold at the Blue Last Tavern, in London, and soon crept into popularity.

FEEDING THE BEER. Managing so that there shall be some saccharine left to cause a slight fermentation, which gives an addition of alcohol and carbonic acid.

FERMENTATION. An act of God, helped by a little yeast, that prohibitionists, members of the W. C. T. U., and other gloom-creators, would like to restrain the Divinity from using.

FINING. To clear cloudy beers and ales containing sediment in suspension. The beer is said to be "fine" when all cloudiness is dispersed.

FIRKIN. A liquid measure of ale and beer containing 9 Imperial or 10.8 U. S. gallons. Anciently it was much larger, being fixed in 1423 at 84 gallons.

FOXING. Also called "bucking," is a disease of malt fermentation that taints beer. It arises from dirty utensils; putting separate worts together in vessels not too deep; using bad malt; by turning on the liquors at too great heats, and brewing in too hot weather. It renders the beer ropy and viscid, like treacle, and soon turns it sour.

FRETTING. A slight fermentation, by which the beer becomes again turbid.

GAMBRINUS. The Teutonic patron saint of brewing. Ganbrivius, otherwise Jean Sans Peur (1371-1419) was said to have been the inventor of hopped malt beer. Gambrinus is also said to be a corruption of Jan Primus, a Burgundian prince, to whom the invention of hopped beer has also been ascribed.

GIN. The essential ingredient of most cocktails. It is also drunk in highballs, punches, rickies, Tom Collinses, and other drinks. Many individuals with no sense of taste even drink it straight, a habit once peculiar to our colored brethren and to London char-women. Gin is the cheapest and most plentiful of our hard liquors, and if you don't let your imagination start to wonder where and how it was made, it can be imbibed with comparative ease. Gin has done much to promote the gay spontaneity and informality that are such delightful features of our American life. Three shots of the average bathtub or homemade gin and Aunt Matilda will start telling the minister shady stories.

GOODS. The brewer's term for the ground malt in the mash tub.

GRIST. Malt that has been ground for mashing.

GUILE. 1. The material for fermenting. 2. The quantity of ale or beer brewed at once. 3. A brewing vat.

GYLE TUN, the fermenting tun, or fermenting tub. The vessel in which the fermentation is carried on. This is also called the working tun, and by the great brewers it is called *squares,* from their form.

HALLYMETER. An instrument for determining the percentage of water in beer by its capacity for dissolving salt.

HANGOVER. The sad and painful feelings on "the morning after the night before." The reason why manufacturers of bromo-seltzer and headache tablets have stayed in business. The one thing that makes you think there *might* be something in not drinking, after all!

HEAVINESS. A lack of carbonic acid in the ale or beer, but containing more alcohol.

HIGHJACKING. An amusing game of thief-rob-thief, often played with the help of machine guns. What's a dead bootlegger more or less among highjackers?

HOGSHEAD. A cask holding 63 gallons.

INHIBITIONS. Peculiar quirks of character that prevent our undressing in public, breaking eggs on bald heads, pinching or kissing every pretty girl we see, and doing the other reprehensible acts we all have the urge to do on occasion. Dr. Freud says we should visit a psychoanalyst and have our inhibitions removed. I can tell you a cheaper and much pleasanter way to remove them: just spend two dòllars for a bottle of gin and go to a Greenwich Village party.

JERSEY-LIGHTNING. See *Apple-Jack*.

KICK. A slang expression, fast becoming reputable, for the alcoholic content in liquor, and its effect. There was a time when wines, beers, and spirits were judged by other qualities than that of how soon they made you turn handsprings, break up your host's furniture, and make advances to your neighbor's wife. Now that is the only thing that counts. If your liquor lacks kick you had best pour it down the sink instead of offering it to your friends.

KILN. An oven or other apparatus, usually constructed of brick, for hardening or drying anything by means of heat.

KRAUSSEN. The billowy mass of foam that rises to the surface of fermenting beer. The same as *cauliflower-head*.

KRAUSENING. The enlivening of beer from which carbonic acid gas has escaped during fining by the addition of one-fifth new beer and four-fifths old beer, thus producing further fermentation.

LAGER. A lightly hopped beer, kept for some months before being used. Fermentation lasted from four to six months at low temperatures of 40° to 60°. Lager means "to store." It has long been popular in Germany, and, before prohibition, was the leading drink of the United States, into which it was introduced in 1842. Lager was "the beer that made Milwaukee famous." American lager also known as *stock beer,* contained about 3.85% of alcohol.

LENGTHS. a. Term used by the brewer to express the whole quantity of one kind of wort made from a certain quantity of malt. b. Making up lengths. Making up the whole quantity of beer of a certain strength.

LIQUOR. In brewing, the water which is used in making wort. Generally speaking, however, liquor is used as a term for all so-called intoxicating beverages. Liquor lubricates the inner man as oil does machinery, and many contend that liquor is as essential to the one as oil is to the other. It is certain that those who hate good liquor have grave defects in their own mechanisms, and are anxious·to ruin the internal workings of more fortunate men. Liquor quickens the mind and stimulates the imagination, an impossibility for those doleful mouth-washes containing "less than one-half of one per cent of alcohol." Without liquor we would soon become a race of gloomy-gusses, about as fit for human association as are a herd of buffalos.

MACE ALE. An ale sweetened and flavored with mace and other spice.

MALT. a. *Pale malt.* Malt which has been exposed to slight heat only in the kiln. b. *Amber malt.* Malt which has been exposed to a degree of heat somewhat greater. c. *Brown malt.* Malt which has been dried so much as to change the color of the grain a little. d. *Patent malt.* Malt that has been roasted like coffee. e. *Slack-dried malt.* Malt which has been dried in the kiln less than usual. f. *Mellowed malt.* That which has been exposed to the air for some time, and which, consequently, has imbibed some water hygrometrically, in contradistinction to that which is fresh from the kiln.

MÜNCHENER. Munich beer, the Bavarian type of lager, with a sweet malt taste, dark color, no strong flavor of hops, and generally lively and sparkling.

MUSTY. A drink once well-known in New England. It was made of ale and lager beer mixed in equal parts.

NEEDLE BEER. A terrible imitation of a real brew made by "spiking" de-alcoholized near-bear. "Spiking" is accomplished by adding raw alcohol, and sometimes ether. Needle beer was common in the early days of prohibition, but is gradually being succeeded by more reputable brews. The taste of needle beer is bad enough, but oy, yoy! *what* a head you have after drinking much of it!

OCTOBER ALE. The old English farmers brewed only twice a year, in October and March, when the temperature was moderate and suitable for fermentation.

PALE ALE. An ale made from malt dried at a low temperature and while fermenting not allowed to rise above 72°.

PILSENER. The Bohemian type of lager beer, having a bitter taste with a pronounced hop flavor, light color, and generally lively and sparkling.

PITCH. To innoculate the brewing with yeast.

PORTER. A very dark, fairly strong English beer, so named because it was first drunk by porters and other hard-working men of London. See *Entire*.

PROHIBITION AGENT. One of the new rich whose fortune has been made since the war. There are so many opportunities for bright young men in this profession it is surprising that a boy even dreams of becoming anything else. Think of it! Wine, women, and song, and all at government expense, plus a salary and—ahem! —little presents one can't refuse. And then sailors have the nerve to ask you to "join the navy and see the world!"

PUNCHEON. A liquor cask of variable capacity, from 72 to 120 gallons.

PURL. A variety of amber beer formerly in great demand in London but now obsolete. Also the name of a mixed drink.

QUARF. A Russian beer made from rye.

QUATERN. A quarter of a gill.

RACKING. The drawing off of liquor from a cask in such a way that the lees, or dregs, are left behind.

RACKETEERS. A group of citizens who are vehemently opposed to modification or repeal of the prohibition laws. The men who control America's best paying industry—the liquor traffic. They have made the residents of Chicago develop a decided distaste for "pine-apples."

ROUNDS. Large vessels like hogsheads, in which brewers transfer the porter from the fermenting vats, to undergo the slow fermentation previous to its being put into the store vats.

SCHENK BEER. A beer fermented in from four to six weeks and brewed for immediate use in winter. Named from the necessity of putting it on schenk (draft) as soon as it is made.

STILLIONS. Vessels to receive the yeast that drains from the barrels; this name is also applied to the supports of the barrels.

STOMACH. A strange cant term used by the workmen for the spiritous odour perceived in fermentation.

STOUT. A dark-colored, malt-flavored beer with a tart taste when properly aged. It is largely brewed in and near Dublin.

TUN. A cask holding 4 hogsheads, or 252 gallons.

TWOPENNY. An amber beer, containing liquorice and capsicum, used as a stimulant in cold weather. The advent of porter sounded the death knell of twopenny.

WEISS. A light, whitish German beer with no strong hop or malt flavor, generally tart and lively, but not brilliant. It is usually brewed from wheat.

WATER. A liquid used for washing and cooking, and as a constituent of beverages. Some people are rash enough to drink water unadulterated, a most dangerous habit when you reflect how it can rust the strongest iron. Think, then, what it must do to the delicate tissues of the human system. If you cannot get wine, whiskey, beer, gin, tea, or, coffee, then, and then only, are you justified in risking your health by taking a very little water. But drink of it sparingly and cease its use as soon as you can get pure, healthful liquor containing enough alcohol to help Nature restore the outraged body to its normal condition.

WEIGHTS AND MEASURES. For rapid conversion of weights and measures the following tables will be found useful:

THIMBLEFUL = 30 *drops*
TEASPOONFUL = 60 *drops*
DESSERT-SPOONFUL = 2 *fluid drachms* (½ *ounce*)
TUMBLERFUL = 8 *fluid ounces* (½ *pint*)
4 GILLS, OR NOGGINS = 1 *pint*
2 PINTS = 1 *quart*
4 QUARTS = 1 *gallon*
31 GALLONS = 1 *barrel*
63 GALLONS = 1 *hogshead*
126 GALLONS = 1 *pipe*, or *butt*
252 GALLONS = 1 *tun*

APOTHECARIES' WEIGHT

20 GRAINS = 1 *scruple*
3 SCRUPLES = 1 *drachm*
8 DRACHMS = 1 *ounce*

AVOIRDUPOIS WEIGHT

16 DRACHMS = 1 *ounce*
16 OUNCES = 1 *pound*

8 QUARTS (DRY MEASURE) = 1 *peck*
4 PECKS = 1 *bushel*
8 BUSHELS = 1 *quarter*
PINCH OF HERBS = 1 *drachm*
HANDFUL = 10 *drachms*

YEAST-BITTER. When too much yeast has been used, and the beer
is rendered too bitter.